Spiritual Fitness and Resilience

A Review of Relevant Constructs, Measures, and Links to Well-Being

Douglas Yeung, Margret T. Martin

RAND Project AIR FORCE

Prepared for the United States Air Force
Approved for public release; distribution unlimited

The research described in this report was sponsored by the United States Air Force under Contract FA7014-06-C-0001. Further information may be obtained from the Strategic Planning Division, Directorate of Plans, Hq USAF.

Library of Congress Controk Number: 2013950810

ISBN: 978-0-8330-7931-2

The RAND Corporation is a nonprofit institution that helps improve policy and decisionmaking through research and analysis. RAND's publications do not necessarily reflect the opinions of its research clients and sponsors.

Support RAND—make a tax-deductible charitable contribution at www.rand.org/giving/contribute.html

RAND® is a registered trademark.

RAND OFFICES
SANTA MONICA, CA • WASHINGTON, DC
PITTSBURGH, PA • NEW ORLEANS, LA • JACKSON, MS • BOSTON, MA
DOHA, QA • CAMBRIDGE, UK • BRUSSELS, BE
www.rand.org

Preface

U.S. military personnel have been engaged in operations in Central Asia and the Middle East for the past decade. Members of the armed forces also deploy to other regions of the world. Many aspects of deployments have the potential to contribute to individual stress, such as uncertainty about deployment time lines; culture shock in theater; fear of or confrontation with death or physical injury; environmental challenges, such as extreme climates and geographical features; austere living conditions; separation from friends and family members; and reintegration after deployment. Service members and their families also manage other military-related stressors, such as frequent relocations, long work hours, and the additional family separations associated with unaccompanied tours and domestic training exercises. Some service members and their families may cope well or even thrive as they overcome adversity and accomplish challenging tasks. However some may suffer negative consequences as a result of military-related stressors, such as physical injury, including traumatic brain injury; depression, anxiety, or other mood disorders; posttraumatic stress disorder; spiritual crises; substance abuse; family dysfunction; marital problems and dissolutions; social isolation; and, in extreme cases, even suicide or suicide attempts. With the aim of preventing such deleterious outcomes, rather than simply responding to them, the study of resilience is of paramount importance.

The Air Force offices of Airman and Family Services (AF/A1S), the Surgeon General (AF/SG), and the Secretary of the Air Force, Force Management and Personnel (SAF/MRM) asked the RAND Corporation to help the Air Force develop its programs to promote resiliency among military and civilian Air Force personnel and their families. This report is one in a series of nine reports that resulted from that research effort.

The overarching report, *Airman and Family Resilience: Lessons from the Scientific Literature* (Meadows and Miller, forthcoming), provides an introduction to resilience concepts and research, documents established and emerging Air Force resiliency efforts, and reviews Air Force metrics for tracking the resiliency of Air Force personnel and their families. It also provides recommendations to support the development of resilience initiatives across the Air Force. We use the term *resilience* to refer to the ability to withstand, recover from, and grow in the face of stressors and *fitness*, which is related, as a "state of adaptation in balance with the conditions at hand" (Mullen, 2010).

Accompanying that overarching report are eight supplemental reports that outline the constructs, metrics, and influential factors relevant to resiliency across the eight domains of Total Force Fitness:

- medical
- nutritional
- environmental
- physical
- social
- spiritual
- behavioral
- psychological.

These supplemental reports are not intended to be a comprehensive review of the entire literature within a domain. Rather, they focus on studies that consider the stress-buffering aspects of each domain, regardless of whether the term *resilience* is specifically used. This expanded the scope of the reviews to include a broader range of applicable studies and also allowed for terminology differences that occur across different disciplines (e.g., stress management, hardiness).

In this report, we identify key constructs relevant to spiritual fitness from the scientific literature: a spiritual worldview, personal religious or spiritual practices and rituals, support from a spiritual community, and spiritual coping. This review includes construct measures as well as well-being and resilience outcomes. We also review interventions designed to promote those spiritual fitness constructs applicable at the individual, unit, family, and community levels.

The results of these reports should be relevant to Air Force leaders who are tasked with monitoring and supporting the well-being of active duty, reserve, and guard Airmen and Air force civilian employees, as well as their families. The results of our studies may also help broaden the scope of research on resilience and help Airmen and their families achieve optimal spiritual fitness.

The research described in this report was conducted within the Manpower, Personnel, and Training Program of RAND Project AIR FORCE as part of a fiscal year 2011 study titled "Program and Facility Support for Air Force Personnel and Family Resiliency."

RAND Project AIR FORCE

RAND Project AIR FORCE (PAF), a division of the RAND Corporation, is the U.S. Air Force's federally funded research and development center for studies and analyses. PAF provides the Air Force with independent analyses of policy alternatives affecting the development, employment, combat readiness, and support of current and future air, space, and cyber forces. Research is conducted in four programs: Force Modernization and Employment; Manpower, Personnel, and Training; Resource Management; and Strategy and Doctrine.

Additional information about PAF is available on our website:
http://www.rand.org/paf/

Contents

Summary

For many people, spiritual beliefs may tremendously influence their outlook on the world, offer solace in turbulent times, or provide support from a like-minded community. These beliefs may thus contribute to resilience and well-being and result in improved force readiness and performance. This report discusses spiritual fitness as defined by the Air Force and as conceptualized by the empirical literature. We first explored how spiritual fitness has been measured. The Army's Global Assessment Tool is one of the few spirituality metrics to focus on service members. Next, we identified key constructs of spiritual fitness, their relationship to well-being and resilience, and interventions that attempted to address these.

First, most spirituality literature includes a conceptualization of a spiritual worldview that includes beliefs in transcendent meaning and purpose, which also include, but are not limited to, organized religious beliefs. Possessing a sense of meaning and purpose in life is strongly positively related to quality of life. Second, personal religious and spiritual practices are linked to improved health and functioning (e.g., protective against substance use). Spiritual meditation may also help improve health (e.g., pain tolerance, buffer physiological stress). Third, there is indirect but converging evidence that support from a spiritual community is generally beneficial to health and well-being. Finally, spiritual coping that is related to purpose in life (i.e., using spiritual beliefs to cope with stressors) drives post-traumatic growth and improved well-being, as opposed to coping that is more narrowly religious. However, spiritual coping is not necessarily effective in coping with such physical stressors as pain. Several constructs of spiritual fitness may be linked to suicidality, such as religious affiliation.

Many of the spiritual interventions and empirical evidence we identified were programs that focused on providing a sense of purpose in life. Although these studies' research designs ranged from observational correlational studies to fully randomized clinical trials, we found diverse types of spiritual interventions that were linked to improved resilience and well-being. Finally, the importance of cultural appropriateness was also very apparent in this literature. Going forward, it will be important to understand how to support not only individuals of, for example, diverse race/ethnicity but also secular individuals as well as Airmen and families within the major religious traditions.

Acknowledgments

This research was sponsored by the Air Force Resilience office and was led by Mr. Brian P. Borda for a significant portion of the study period and by Air Force Surgeon General Lt Gen (Dr.) Charles B. Green, and Mr. William H. Booth, the Assistant Secretary of the Air Force for Manpower and Reserve Affairs (SAF/MRM).

We would like to thank the action officers from the sponsoring offices for their role in shaping the research agenda and providing feedback on interim and final briefings of the research findings. Those officers are Maj Kirby Bowling, our primary contact from the Air Force Resilience office; Col John Forbes and Lt Col David Dickey from the Air Force Surgeon General's office; and Ms. Linda Stephens-Jones from SAF/MRM. We also appreciate the insights and recommendations received from Ms. Eliza Nesmith while she was in the Air Force Services and from Lt Col Shawn Campbell while he served in the SAF/MRM office.

RAND's Sarah Meadows and Laura Miller led the overall research effort on resilience and provided extensive feedback on a previous draft of this manuscript. Donna White and Hosay Salam Yaqub provided valuable assistance formatting the manuscript and assembling the bibliography. Finally, we acknowledge our reviewers, Dr. Kenneth Pargament and Dr. Rajeev Ramchand, for their thoughtful reviews, which greatly improved this report.

Abbreviations

Bio-PSSI	BIOPsychoSocioSpiritual Inventory
CSI-MEMO	Comfort, Stress, Influence-Member, Other (spiritual history tool for clinicians)
DBT	dialectical behavior therapy
DoD	Department of Defense
DSES	Daily Spiritual Experience Scale
EPP	Eight-Point Programme
FACIT-Sp	Functional Assessment of Chronic Illness Therapy–Spiritual Well-Being
FACT	Faith, Active (or Available, Accessible, Applicable), Coping (or Comfort, Conflicts, Concerns), Treatment (spiritual history tool for clinicians)
FICA	Faith, Importance or Influence, Community, Address/Action (spiritual history tool)
GAT	Global Assessment Tool
HOPE	Hope, Organized, Personal, Effects (questions for spiritual assessment)
MFQ	Moral Foundation Questionnaire
PAF	Project AIR FORCE
PTSD	post-traumatic stress disorder
rCOPE	Religious Coping Methods Measure
RSES	Response to Stressful Experiences Scale
SBI-15R	Systems of Belief Inventory
SIBS	Spiritual Involvement and Beliefs Scale
SPIRIT	Spiritual, Personal, Integration, Ritualized, Implications, Terminal (spiritual history mnemonic)
SRA	Self-Report Altruism Scale
SWBS	Spiritual Well-Being Scale
TCI	Temperament and Character Inventory

1. The Context of This Report[1]

This report is one of a series designed to support Air Force leaders in promoting resilience among Airmen, its civilian employees, and Air Force family members. The research sponsors requested that RAND assess the current resilience-related constructs and measures in the scientific literature and report any evidence of initiatives that promote resilience across a number of domains. We did not limit our search to research conducted in military settings or with military personnel, as Air Force leaders sought the potential opportunity to apply the results of these studies to a population that had not yet been addressed (i.e., Airmen). Further, many Air Force services support Air Force civilians and family members, and thus the results of civilian studies would apply to these populations.

This study adopts the Air Force definition of resilience: "the ability to withstand, recover and/or grow in the face of stressors and changing demands," which we found to encompass a range of definitions of resilience given throughout the scientific literature.[2] By focusing on resilience, the armed forces aim to expand their care to ensure the well-being of military personnel and their families through preventative measures and not just by treating members after they begin to experience negative outcomes (e.g., depression, anxiety, insomnia, substance abuse, post-traumatic stress disorder, or suicidal ideation).

Admiral Michael Mullen, Chairman of the Joint Chiefs of Staff from 2007 to 2011, outlined the Total Force Fitness (TFF) concept in a special issue of the journal *Military Medicine*: "A total force that has achieved total fitness is healthy, ready, and resilient; capable of meeting challenges and surviving threats" (Mullen, 2010, p. 1). This notion of "fitness" is directly related to the concept of resilience. The same issue of *Military Medicine* also reflected the collective effort of scholars, health professionals, and military personnel, who outlined eight domains of TFF: medical, nutritional, environmental, physical, social, spiritual, behavioral, and psychological. This framework expands on the traditional conceptualization of resilience by looking beyond the psychological realm to also emphasize the mind-body connection and the interdependence of each of the eight domains.

---

[1] Adapted from Meadows and Miller, forthcoming.

[2] The Air Force adopted this definition, which was developed by the Defense Centers of Excellence for Psychological Health and Traumatic Brain Injury (DCoE, 2011).

The research sponsors requested that RAND adopt these eight fitness domains as the organizing framework for our literature review. We followed this general framework, although in some cases we adapted the scope of a domain to better reflect the relevant research. Thus, this study resulted in eight reports, each focusing on resilience-related research in one of the TFF domains, but we note that not all of these domains are mutually exclusive. These eight reports define each domain and address the following interrelated topics:

- medical: preventive care, the presence and management of injuries, chronic conditions, and barriers and bridges to accessing appropriate quality health care (Shih, Meadows, and Martin, 2013)
- nutritional: food intake, dietary patterns and behavior, and the food environment (Flórez, Shih, and Martin, forthcoming)
- environmental: environmental stressors and potential workplace injuries and preventive and protective factors (Shih, Meadows, Mendeloff, and Bowling, forthcoming)
- physical: physical activity and fitness (Robson, 2013)
- social: social fitness and social support from family, friends, coworkers/unit members, neighbors, and cyber communities (McGene, 2013)
- spiritual: spiritual worldview, personal religious or spiritual practices and rituals, support from a spiritual community, and and spiritual coping (Yeung and Martin, 2013)
- behavioral: health behaviors related to sleep and to drug, alcohol, and tobacco use (Robson and Salcedo, forthcoming)
- psychological: self-regulation, positive and negative affect, perceived control, self-efficacy, self-esteem, optimism, adaptability, self-awareness, and emotional intelligence (Robson, forthcoming).

These reports are not intended to be comprehensive reviews of the entire literature within a domain. Rather, they focus on those studies that consider the stress-buffering aspects of each domain, regardless of whether the term *resilience* is specifically used. This expanded the scope of the reviews to include a broader range of studies and also allowed for differences in the terminology used across different disciplines (e.g., stress management, hardiness). We sought evidence both on the main effects of resilience factors in each domain (i.e., those that promote general well-being) and on the indirect or interactive effects (i.e., those that buffer the negative effects of stress).

Because the Air Force commissioned this research to specifically address individuals' capacity to be resilient, and thus their well-being, our reports do not address whether or how fitness in each of the eight TFF domains could be linked to other outcomes of interest to the military, such as performance, military discipline, unit readiness, personnel costs, attrition, or retention. Those worthy topics were beyond the scope of this project.

Some other important parameters shaped this literature review. First, across the study, we focused on research from the past decade, although older studies are included, particularly landmark studies that still define the research landscape or where a particular line of inquiry has been dormant in recent years. Second, we prioritized research on adults in the United States. Research on children was included where particularly germane (e.g., in discussions of family as a form of social support), and, occasionally, research on adults in other Western nations is referenced or subsumed within a large study. Research on elderly populations was generally excluded. Third, we prioritized literature reviews, meta-analyses, and on-going bodies of research over more singular smaller-scale studies.

The search for evidence on ways to promote resilience in each domain included both actions that individuals could take as well as actions that organizations could take, such as information campaigns, policies, directives, programs, initiatives, facilities, or other resources. We did not filter out evidence related to Air Force practices already under way, as the Air Force was interested both in research related to existing practices and in research that might suggest new paths for promoting resilience. Our aim was not to collect examples of creative or promising initiatives at large but to seek scholarly publications assessing the stress-buffering capacity of initiatives. Thus, in general, this collection of reviews does not address initiatives that have not yet been evaluated for their effect.

Building on the foundation of the eight reports that assess the scientific literature in each domain, RAND prepared an overarching report that brings together the highlights of these reviews and examines their relevance to current Air Force metrics and programs. That ninth report, *Airman and Family Resilience: Lessons from the Scientific Literature,* provides a more in-depth introduction to resilience concepts and research, presents our model of the relationship between resilience and TFF, documents established and emerging Air Force resiliency efforts, and reviews the Air Force metrics for tracking the resiliency of Air Force personnel and their families. By comparing the information we found in the research literature to Air Force practices, we were able to provide recommendations to support the development of initiatives to promote resilience across the Air Force. Although the overview report contains Air Force-specific recommendations that take into account all eight domains and existing Air Force practices, some are applicable to the military more generally and are highlighted at the end of this report.

2. Spiritual Fitness Definition and Key Constructs

"Man never made any material as resilient as the human spirit."
— Bern Williams, Author

"If in normal conditions it is skill, which counts, in such extreme situations, it is the spirit, which saves."

— Walter Bonatti, Mountain Climber

The importance of certain fitness domains, such as physical and psychological fitness, is intuitive, but it is not immediately apparent how spiritual fitness may be beneficial for Air Force readiness and resilience. Yet, for many people, spiritual beliefs influence their outlook on the world tremendously, offer solace in turbulent times, and provide support from a like-minded community. These beliefs may thus contribute to resilience and well-being and result in improved force readiness and performance. This report discusses spiritual fitness as defined by the Air Force and as conceptualized by the empirical literature. We identify key constructs of spiritual fitness and their relationship to well-being and resilience. We then review evidence regarding the efficacy of spiritual interventions targeting these spiritual fitness constructs.

Definition

The Air Force defines spiritual fitness as *the ability to adhere to beliefs, principles, or values needed to persevere and prevail in accomplishing missions.* As this definition implies, spiritual fitness does not require any degree of religiosity or belief in the supernatural. Atheists who hold a secular philosophy of meaning and purpose can be spiritually fit as well. Spiritual fitness can come in many forms and may include any of the following: belief in transcendent meaning and purpose, self-transcendence, a sense of morality, engagement with a community with similar values, altruism, religiosity, religious or spiritual practices or behaviors, or exceptional experiences, such as visions or perceived communications with the deceased.[3] An article in a special issue of the journal *Military Medicine* on the Total Force Fitness model (Jonas et al., 2010) defined the spiritual fitness domain as "fitness of the spirit or soul, especially from a religious aspect" (Hufford, Fritts, and Rhodes, 2010). To avoid the appearance that the Department of

---

[3] See Hood, 1975, for an example of a scale designed to measure such exceptional experiences.

Defense (DoD) was advocating policies that favor one spiritual tradition over another, the article's authors focused on "psychospiritual fitness"—the overarching realm where spirituality intersects with the psychological domain. In this report, we define spiritual fitness as the capacity for adherence to core personal values (i.e., a belief system) that reflect beliefs in transcendent or ultimate meaning and purpose. This definition extends beyond the Air Force's definition by including concepts of transcendence and ultimate meaning, which are also related to the concept of the sacred (Pargament, 2007).

To explore the spiritual domain, we consulted the literature on spirituality in a clinical context as well as research linking spirituality to resiliency and well-being. We included research that explores how religious beliefs and practices influence coping and well-being and excluded research on religion or spirituality independent of any association with stress or well-being. We also did not focus on research that explores any particular religion in depth, although we do provide an occasional example from these studies but only for illustrative purposes. Although research focused on religiosity has demonstrated some links to mental and physical health, these studies have typically assessed religion only in terms of particular religious affiliations (Storch et al., 2004).

In the sections that follow, we first review prominent measures of spiritual fitness. Next, we describe the key constructs of spiritual fitness that we identified, including relevant metrics and resilience and well-being outcomes. We briefly discuss evidence relating these key constructs to suicidal behavior, given the importance of that topic to the military. Finally, we describe various spiritual fitness interventions and evidence regarding their effectiveness.

Key Constructs and Metrics of Spiritual Fitness

We identified four major constructs relevant to spiritual fitness: (1) spiritual worldview, (2) personal religious or spiritual practices and rituals, (3) support from a spiritual community, and (4) spiritual coping. Research has linked these spiritual fitness constructs to various aspects of well-being, such as improved quality of life and physical and mental health. In addition, these constructs—spiritual worldview and spiritual coping in particular—may also indirectly affect various well-being outcomes by buffering stress.

Prominent Metrics of Spiritual Fitness Related to Key Constructs

Research on these key constructs shows that numerous metrics of religiosity and spirituality are related to spiritual fitness. Table 2.1 describes the prominent metrics of spiritual fitness that relate to our key constructs. Although most of these metrics relate to more than one construct, we attempted to group each according to its primary or major

Table 2.1
Spiritual Fitness Metrics

A. Measures of Spiritual Worldview (e.g., life's purpose and meaning, transcendence, and personal values)				
Name of Measure	**Description**	**Reliability**	**Validity**	**Citation**
HOPE*	This measure was designed as a teaching tool to help medical professionals integrate a spiritual assessment into a medical interview. Its 20 questions are intended to cover basic areas of inquiry: H (sources of hope, meaning, comfort, strength, peace, love, and connection); O (organized religion); P (personal spirituality and practices); E (effects on medical care and end-of-life issues.	Not available because this is a structured interview that aims for open-ended rather than quantitative answers.	Not validated in initial citation	Anandarajah and Hight, 2001
FACIT-Sp	This measure contains 12 items and is illness-specific. It was designed to measure important aspects of spirituality, such as a sense of meaning and purpose in life and sense of strength of comfort.	Internal consistency for the overall scale was .87, and from .81 to .87 for each of the two factors (faith, and meaning/peace).	Spirituality, as measured by FACIT-Sp, was associated with quality of life to the same degree as physical well-being, which is "unquestioned in its importance" to quality of life.	Brady et al., 1999

Table 2.1—Continued

A. Measures of Spiritual Worldview (e.g., life's purpose and meaning, transcendence, and personal values)				
Name of Measure	Description	Reliability	Validity	Citation
TCI	The Self-Transcendence character scale. Three factors in the scale include (1) self-forgetful vs. self-conscious (11 items), (2) transpersonal identification (9 items), and (3) spiritual acceptance vs. materialism (13 items).	Internal consistency for the three subscales ranges from .72 to .74.	Self-transcendence was found to be useful in differentiating schizoid from schizotypal patients because "the latter tend to endorse questions about extrasensory perception and other aspects of self-transcendence."	Cloninger, Svrakic, and Przybeck, 1993
Bio-PSSI	One of the five scales in this measure is the seven-item spiritual symptom scale, which concerns peace, harmony, and purpose.	The scales (including spiritual symptoms) are correlated with relevant diagnoses, medications, and health care use. Internal consistency is high (α = .862-.967).	Spiritual symptoms are identified (which assess, for example, purpose in life) associated with life lacking meaning (β = 1.214, $p < .001$)	Katerndahl, 2008

Table 2.1—Continued

A. Measures of Spiritual Worldview (e.g., life's purpose and meaning, transcendence, and personal values)				
Name of Measure	Description	Reliability	Validity	Citation
Spiritual Orientation Inventory	This 85-item measure of "humanistic spirituality" is not necessarily affiliated with traditional religious beliefs or practices. Nine subscales include Transcendent Dimension, Meaning and Purpose, Mission in Life, Sacredness of Life, Material Values, Altruism, Idealism, Awareness of the Tragic, and Fruits of Spirituality.	Internal consistency for the nine subscales ranges from .75 to .95.	Earlier versions of the scale (1) included a large number of items, drawn from previous spirituality scales and a literature review, which were selected and rated by experts, and (2) were used to identify individuals nominated by a panel as "highly spiritual." The overall scale and eight of nine subscales successfully identified "highly spiritual" people.	Elkins et al., 1988
SIBS	This 26-item measure was designed to be a comprehensive and widely applicable instrument to help (1) physicians conduct quantitative spiritual assessment of patients and (2) facilitate the study of patient spirituality in medical care.	Internal consistency is .92; test-retest reliability is .92.	The measure has a strong correlation (.80) with the Spiritual Well-Being Scale (see below).	Hatch et al., 1998

Table 2.1—Continued

	A. Measures of Spiritual Worldview (e.g., life's purpose and meaning, transcendence, and personal values)			
Name of Measure	**Description**	**Reliability**	**Validity**	**Citation**
SWBS	This 20-item scale assesses well-being in terms of spirituality.	Reliability scores are reported in several sources. For example, Riley et al. (1998) reported internal consistency as .87 and test-retest reliability as .93. Scott, Agresti, and Fitchett (1998) report several similarly high-reliability scores.	The measure has a normal distribution of scores when tested on clinical populations (Scott, Agresti, and Fitchett, 1998).	Paloutzian and Ellison, 1982
MFQ	This 30-item scale is designed to measure the full range of moral concerns. (There is also a 20-item, short-form MFQ.)	Internal consistency for the five subscales ranged from .65-.84. Test-retest reliability for the five subscales ranged from .68-.82.	Correlations between subscales and other conceptually related scales averaged .51. MFQ also predicted attitudes toward various social groups.	Graham et al., 2011
SRA	This 20-item scale is used to broadly measure the trait of altruism.	Internal consistency was .89.	Correlation with peer ratings of altruism was .35. SRA also predicted other measures of altruism.	Rushton, Chrisjohn, and Fekken, 1981

Table 2.1—Continued

B. Measures of Personal Religious or Spiritual Practices					
Name of Measure	**Description**	**Reliability**	**Validity**	**Other**	**Citation**
SPIRIT*	This is a 22-question interviewing tool to aid physicians in spiritual history-taking. Mnemonic components include spiritual belief system, personal spirituality, integration with a spiritual community, ritualized practices and restrictions, Implications for medical care, and terminal events planning.				Maugans, 1996
FICA	This is an 11-question spiritual assessment tool for clinical settings. Components include faith, belief, meaning; importance and Influence; community; and address in care.		Quantitative ratings and qualitative comments are correlated with spiritual items from a quality-of-life (QOL) scale (City of Hope-QOL Tool; Ferrell et al., 1995).		Borneman, Ferrell, and Puchalski, 2010
FACIT-Sp					See above.
DSES	This scale contains 16 items (a six-item version is used in the General Social Survey). It addresses reported ordinary experiences of spirituality such as awe, joy that lifts one out of the mundane, and a sense of deep inner peace.	Across several studies, internal consistency estimates are in the .90s.	Preliminary construct validity was assessed by comparing against expected correlations for demographic subgroups and health and quality-of-life indicators.	Several questions refer directly to an individual's (presumed) relationship with God.	Underwood and Teresi, 2002

11

Table 2.1—Continued

C. Measures of Religious Coping					
Name of Measure	**Description**	**Reliability**	**Validity**	**Other**	**Citation**
SBI-15R					See below.
rCOPE	This is a 21-item measure of positive and negative patterns of religious coping methods.	Internal consistency for the positive and negative scale was moderate to high across several separate studies.	Positive and negative scales were uncorrelated or only slightly correlated (.17) across several separate studies. Each scale exhibited different patterns of correlations with other measures.	The scale distinguishes religious coping that has either positive or negative effects. Also contains explicitly religious items/factors.	Pargament et al., 1998
FICA					See above.
FACT*	This is a spiritual history tool for clinicians. Components include Faith (or beliefs), Active (or Available, Accessible, Applicable), Coping (or Comfort), Treatment plan.			The tool claims to be comparable and possibly more effective because the spiritual history tools are chaplain- rather than physician-developed.	LaRocca-Pitts, 2008
CSI-MEMO	This measure includes Comfort (provided by religious beliefs), Stress (provided by religious beliefs), spiritual beliefs that might Influence medical decisions, Member of a religious or spiritual community and whether it is supportive, and Other spiritual needs that someone should address.				Koenig, 2002

Table 2.1—Continued

	C. Measures of Religious Coping				
Name of Measure	Description	Reliability	Validity	Other	Citation
FACIT-Sp					See above.
RSES	This 22-item scale provides a brief, reliable, and valid measure of individual differences in cognitive, emotional, and behavioral responses to life's most stressful events. It is intended to complement existing measures of resilience by providing a measure that focuses on how an individual characteristically responds during and immediately after life's most stressful events. Factor analysis suggested five protective factors: (a) meaning-making and restoration, (b) active coping, (c) cognitive flexibility, (d) spirituality, and (e) self-efficacy.	The scale demonstrated sound internal consistency ($\alpha = 0.91 - 0.93$) and good test-retest reliability ($r = 0.87$).	In separate military samples, the RSES accounted for unique variance in PTSD symptoms above and beyond existing scales measuring resilience-related constructs, thereby demonstrating incremental validity.	The scale was developed using separate military samples.	Johnson et al., 2011

Table 2.1—Continued

D. Measures of Social Support from Spiritual or Religious Community					
Name of Measure	**Description**	**Reliability**	**Validity**	**Other**	**Citation**
FACIT-Sp					See above.
The Perceived Support from God Scale	The scale consists of 15 items in two subscales (Support from God and God's Purpose for Me) and was designed to capture coping strategies that contribute to the psychological well-being of Christian African American cancer survivors.	Internal consistency scores were .94 and .86 for the Support from God and God's Purpose for Me subscales, respectively. Test-retest reliability scores were .94 and .88 for the Support from God and God's Purpose for Me subscales, respectively.	Subscales were moderately to strongly correlated with existing religious involvement and beliefs measures.	The scale was administered to African American cancer survivors.	Hamilton et al., 2010
SBI-15R	This is a 15-item scale of spiritual and religious beliefs and practices and of the social support derived from a spiritual/religious community. Four subscales are Existential, Ritual, Social support, and Being.	Internal consistency for the overall scale was .97, and ranged from .85 to .94 for each of the four subscales. Test-retest reliability was .95.	The scale correlated highly with an expanded version of the SBI created for validation purposes and with other spirituality scales. It is also able to discriminate religious from lay group.	It notes that one important use is differentiating individuals in religious orders from a lay population. It has been translated into Hebrew, German, and Spanish and is available for cross-cultural studies.	Holland et al., 1998

* Indicates structured interviews rather than formal scales.

theme. We also note which of these metrics are structured interview instruments rather than survey scales.

According to Moberg (2005), the Spiritual Well Being Scale (SWBS) (Paloutzian and Ellison, 1982) is the most widely used spirituality instrument. However, it has been criticized for being biased toward Christian religiosity. Scott, Agresti, and Fitchett (1998) note that evangelical Christians often score highest on the SWBS. Indeed, several items refer explicitly to an individual's relationship with God. Another metric that addresses this issue, and which is prototypical of how we defined the spiritual fitness domain, is the Spiritual Involvement and Beliefs Scale (SIBS) (Hatch et al., 1988), designed specifically to be inclusive of spirituality rather than of religiosity. Maltby and Day (2001) argue that SIBS is intended to reflect that "individuals can be very spiritual, without being religious." Another possible concern regarding the SWBS as well as some other metrics (e.g., FACIT-Sp [Functional Assessment of Chronic Illness Therapy–Spiritual Well-Being]) is that they describe constructs that may not necessarily be related to spirituality, such as sense of meaning and purpose, hope, or optimism. Koenig (2008) points out that these constructs are themselves often conceptualized as "well-being," which may render metrics such as the SWBS less useful for measuring spirituality. However, given how frequently such measures are used in spirituality research (e.g., Moberg, 2005), we opted for inclusiveness and referenced these measures in our review.

A new spirituality metric of note is focused on military service members. Because of the First Amendment's Establishment Clause, DoD must not establish religion, but must protect the rights of service members to freely exercise religion. Therefore, it must carefully consider any proposed measures of spirituality for its military population. As part of the recently implemented Comprehensive Soldier Fitness program, the Global Assessment Tool (GAT) is intended to assess Army soldiers across several psychological domains, including spiritual fitness (Peterson, Park, and Castro, 2011). The spiritual fitness component of the GAT primarily measures soldiers' meaning and purpose in life[4] without intending to specifically reference or promote religiousness.[5] In spite of this, or perhaps because of its ambiguous language, the GAT has been criticized as pronouncing soldiers to be spiritually unfit unless they indicate religiousness or spiritual beliefs in some form (Leopold, 2011). Currently, the GAT does not provide a way to link spiritual fitness with key well-being outcomes, such as mental health. Although administering the

---

[4] Note that transcendence, which we define as part of the spiritual worldview that is key to spiritual fitness, is included in the emotional fitness domain of the GAT. However, a single item in the GAT spiritual fitness domain refers to transcendence as we have defined it.

[5] Army lawyers and chaplains were consulted about the appropriateness of spiritual fitness questions (see Peterson, Park, and Castro, 2011).

GAT to a sample of approximately 8,000 soldiers suggested initial reliability and validity, Peterson and colleagues (2011) noted that research using a shortened version to associate GAT scores with concrete indicators of well-being is still in progress.

Several themes emerged among the spirituality metrics we identified. First, there are different types of measurement instruments, with different intended purposes. Besides formal, often more academic, scales, structured interview instruments are used to take "spiritual assessments" or "spiritual histories," generally measuring the same key factors as the scales. Questions about faith or religious beliefs are particularly prevalent in spiritual assessment interviews, and they typically ask whether an individual considers him/herself to be spiritual or religious or has spiritual beliefs[6] (e.g., Borneman, Ferrell, and Puchalski, 2010). Clinicians, physicians, and nurses may use these interview instruments in the course of treatment to gain a greater understanding of the patient's needs, such as their preferences on how their newborn is handled after delivery (see Lewallen, 2009). LaRocca-Pitts (2009) discusses the different levels of qualitative spiritual assessments, which he notes are distinct from quantitative scales of spirituality. At the most basic level, *spiritual screens* seek to determine basic, and presumably unchanging, information about a patient (i.e., faith or religious affiliation and any particular religious or cultural needs). For more detailed information, interviewers may also conduct a *spiritual history*, using either an informal or formal checklist to attempt to determine ways that the patient's spiritual or religious life may affect medical care. Finally, *spiritual assessments* are the most involved form of qualitative measure, taking "an in-depth look at the patient's spiritual makeup with the goal of identifying potential areas of spiritual concern and determining an appropriate treatment plan" (LaRocca-Pitts, 2009).

Second, although spiritual fitness itself is conceptualized to be positive and beneficial, some scales measure the "opposite" of spiritual fitness. In other words, these metrics seek to measure whether individuals are spiritually *un*fit and measure constructs such as spiritual symptoms (e.g., Bio-PSSI [BIOPsychoSocioSpiritual Inventory]; Katerndahl, 2008), spiritual distress and crisis, and adaptive as well as maladaptive religious coping, which has been called "religious struggle" (e.g., rCOPE [Religious Coping Methods Measure]; Pargament et al., 1998).

Third, in addition to the key constructs that constitute spiritual fitness, several spirituality metrics include items relating to medical care planning, especially end-of-life issues and mortality. Metrics with such items include SPIRIT (Spiritual, Personal,

------

[6] In these assessments, the definition of spirituality appears typically to be left to individual patients' interpretations.

Integration Ritualized, Implications, Terminal) (Maugans, 1996), FICA (Faith, Importance or Influence, Community, Address/Action) (Borneman, Ferrell, and Puchalski, 2010), and FACT (Faith, Active [or Available, Accessible, Applicable], Coping [or Comfort, Conflicts, Concerns], Treatment) (LaRocca-Pitts, 2008). With a greater understanding of patients' spiritual needs, health care providers can then incorporate patients' spiritual or religious preferences into end-of-life treatment or initiate conversations that may reveal depression or anxiety.

Finally, some spiritual fitness metrics have been applied to specific demographic groups, such as individuals of a particular race/ethnicity (see Stanard, Sandhu, and Painter, 2000, for several examples). Researchers have therefore sought to determine the appropriateness of these instruments for specific groups, with mixed results. For instance, Sexson (2004) discusses issues in religious/spiritual assessment for children and adolescents and lists some existing scales, noting, however, that most are Christian-focused. Sexson argues that it is better to conduct such assessments for children or adolescents within the context of the family, such as in interviews or observation, rather than merely using scales that may not account for various stages of development. And, recently, specific instruments (both semistructured interviews and scales) were developed to explore the role of spirituality among African Americans with cancer (Holt et al., 2011). Adequate reliability, but only mixed validity, was demonstrated for these measures. Stronger, but initial, support for reliability and validity on an African American population was obtained for another instrument, the Perspectives of Support from God Scale, which is about perceived social support from a religious community (Hamilton et al., 2010). Lewis (2008), however, conducted a meta-analysis of general instruments (e.g., SWBS, FACIT-Sp) that have been used to assess spirituality and health in African Americans. She found that these tools overall were not valid for African Americans because they were missing "distinct cultural attributes of African American spirituality." From this she concluded that the cultural appropriateness of these instruments and studies was generally lacking. Stanard, Sandhu, and Painter (2000) contend that the Spirituality Scale (Jagers and Smith, 1996), which is intended for individuals with an "Afrocultural perspective," appears valid for such use but was not included in Lewis's meta-analysis.

Spiritual Worldview

The Air Force's description of spiritual fitness as a set of core personal values suggests a conceptualization of a spiritual worldview that includes beliefs in transcendent meaning and purpose. This definition reflects the spiritual worldview's prominence in the spirituality literature, much of which includes some notion of core personal values by which individuals derive peace and comfort and a sense of meaning or purpose to life.

Such values include, for example, hope and peace (Anandarajah and Hight, 2001), healing (Danesh, 2008), optimism (Koenig, 2002), morality (Litz et al., 2009), ultimacy (Emmons, 1999), and altruism (Rushton, Chrisjohn, and Fekken, 1981). Self-transcendence is a particularly noteworthy part of the spiritual worldview and refers to the idea that there is something beyond the individual, which can be the interconnectedness and interdependence of humanity, the natural world, or a higher being (Elkins et al., 1998). Cloninger, Svrakic, and Pryzbeck (1993) describe a "unitive consciousness"—an understanding that everything is part of a unified whole. In describing spirituality as "a search for the sacred," Pargament (2008) defines what is sacred as virtually any aspect of life that is related to others and community.

The construct of self-transcendence, therefore, includes, but is not limited to, beliefs in God or beliefs that are related to traditional organized religion (e.g., Hatch et al., 1998). Indeed, self-transcendence is key to spiritual nontheism and similar nonreligious yet spiritual worldviews. Rothman (2009) describes various self-reported conceptions of spirituality that refer to the interconnectedness of life and nature or of human relationships. Transcendence can also be found in "spiritual atheism," in which individuals view themselves as spiritual but not believing in God or a god, often aligning their beliefs and values with science (Ecklund and Long, 2011). Ecklund and Long interviewed scientists from top U.S. research universities. Discussing their beliefs, these scientists described searching for meaning—for a "core sense of truth through spirituality"—and reported feeling transcendence in connection with the natural world.

Particularly relevant for the military, patriotism and various forms of military-related values may also constitute a possible nonreligious type of spirituality. For instance, Moskos's (1977) influential institutional/occupational thesis of military values posits an "institutional" orientation that, in emphasizing sacrifice for the greater good, embodies some of the spiritual elements of transcendence. Indeed, McCloy and Clover (1988) compare the acquisition of institutionalized values in military training—taken to the extreme—to "getting religion." These military values, such as service and sacrifice, appear to be relatively uniform. A survey of student officers in military academies worldwide revealed some national differences but an overall orientation toward these institutional values (Soeters, 1997). Honor is another example of a value that, in a military context, serves as an "incentive" toward altruistic sacrifice (Olsthoorn, 2005). Interestingly, it has been suggested that integrity—commonly cited as a core value in military personnel—may in fact be a problematic virtue in military leadership (Olsthoorn, 2009). This is because, on an individual level, integrity may cause a leader to uphold his or her personal values, even when they conflict with those of the military. Moskos and Wood (1988) point out that leaders must exhibit the goals and values of the institution (i.e., the military), rather than their own individual goals. Demonstrating the institution's values, they argue, is necessary to promote self-sacrifice for the good of the institution and increases organizational commitment and performance.[7]

Metrics. Most spirituality metrics include some aspect of the spiritual worldview construct. Examples of metrics that prominently feature these concepts of purpose, meaning, and transcendence include, for example, TCI (Cloninger et al., 1993), which explores self-transcendence, and HOPE (Anandarajah and Hight, 2001), which also explores individual values of hope, organized religion, personal spirituality, and practices, as well as the effects of these values and beliefs on medical care and end-of-life decisions. Morality is another facet of one's core personal values, which may differ by demographic group. The Moral Foundations Questionnaire (Graham et al., 2011) assesses a wide range of personal moral concerns that could form the foundation of a values-oriented spiritual worldview. This metric may be particularly useful in revealing demographic differences, because it has been administered worldwide as an online survey. Results showed cross-cultural differences (e.g., that individuals in Eastern cultures value in-group concerns more highly than do those in Western cultures) and gender differences (e.g., women value harm, fairness, and purity concerns more highly than do men). Morality and values may also differ by socioeconomic status (Haidt, Koller, and Dias, 1993).

Well-being outcomes. Possessing a spiritual worldview is associated with well-being and general psychological health. Hackney and Sanders (2003) conducted a meta-analysis of 34 religiosity and mental health studies, finding that the most personal manifestations of religious behavior—which they suggested were indicative of deeply held spiritual worldviews—were more strongly related to psychological well-being. Moreira-Almeida, Neto, and Koenig (2006) reviewed 850 religiousness and mental health studies completed after 2000, noting several studies that had found spiritual beliefs to have a positive effect on psychological well-being. Reviewing spirituality literature for individuals with chronic illness, Nichols and Hunt (2011) discuss specific aspects of a spiritual worldview (i.e., transcendence, meaning and purpose in life) and how they are used by individuals with chronic illness.

Several related concepts within the spiritual worldview construct have been linked to well-being. Surveying 1,610 cancer patients, Brady et al. (1999) found that feeling a

---

[7] This potential conflict between individual and organizational goals may not include situations in which the institution encourages or even requires its members to pursue unethical goals. This issue of the proper balance between the values of personal integrity and self-sacrifice for the broader group is complex and deserves further attention, but it is outside the scope of this study. However, this conflict is noteworthy, as the potentially unintended consequence of pursuing spiritual fitness when an individual's beliefs or worldview come into conflict with that of the larger organization.

sense of meaning and purpose was one of the best predictors of "contentment with quality of life." As measured with the FACIT-Sp, spiritual well-being is conceptualized as reflecting "a sense of meaning in one's life, harmony, peacefulness" and is strongly positively related to quality of life (Brady et al., 1999). Spiritual intelligence (i.e., a concern with the fundamental questions in life and how they relate to one's inner and external lives) was strongly positively related to happiness in a descriptive cross-sectional study of Iranian nurses (Faribors, Fatemeh, and Hamidreza, 2010). A series of four correlational samples showed that daily spiritual experiences of transcendence were associated with improved quality of life and psychosocial status (Underwood and Teresi, 2002). Spiritual strivings—that is, when people attempt to achieve spiritual goals—may indicate the extent to which spiritual beliefs are strongly held and integrated into daily life (Emmons, 1999). Emmons found that spiritual strivings were positively correlated with various measures of well-being, including happiness, satisfaction with life, neuroticism, and depression.

On the other hand, lacking a spiritual worldview or violating one's spiritual beliefs may have negative consequences. Nonspiritual well-being—that is, not feeling peace or purpose and meaning in life, or not deriving comfort from a relationship with God—has been associated with lower quality of life and life satisfaction (Riley et al., 1998). Also, an empirical test of the TCI that was administered to 300 adults found that self-transcendence is slightly lower in clinical patients than in the general population (Cloninger, Svrakic, and Przybeck, 1993).[8] Finally, moral injury, which may occur when wartime actions (or even bearing witness to such actions) violate deep moral beliefs, is theorized to diminish psychological and spiritual well-being for veterans (Litz et al., 2009).

The relationship between spiritual beliefs and well-being may also change over the life span, growing stronger in older adults (see Moberg, 2005, for a review). Mabe and Josephson (2004) note the potential, earlier in life, for child psychopathology based on "poorness-of-fit" between family religious beliefs and practices and negative mental health (e.g., families viewing a mentally impaired child as punishment from God).

Resilience outcomes. The search for meaning and purpose may be an important coping mechanism during chronic illness (Nichols and Hunt, 2011). For instance, Smith et al. (2009), using a sample of only women, showed that purpose in life (as well as other resilience factors) is related to greater habituation to painful stimuli. They speculate that possessing this purpose in life may provide motivation to overcome pain or may increase a more general ability to adapt to or cope with stress. Similarly, Emmons (1999) argues

---

[8] This research did not distinguish between patients with personality disorders and those without.

that spiritual beliefs serve as "an integrating and stabilizing force that provides a framework for interpreting life's challenges," in this manner acting as a set of adaptive skills that he refers to as spiritual intelligence. He then suggests that these types of spiritual skills offer people a way to cope with trauma, helping them to focus on what they find truly important in life.

Personal Religious or Spiritual Practices and Rituals

Personal religious or spiritual practices and rituals can serve to demonstrate and reinforce spiritual or religious faith, beliefs, and values (Anandarajah and Hight, 2001; Holland et al., 1998; Maugans, 1996). These practices may include church attendance, prayer, volunteer work, holiday celebrations, rites of passage, meditation, or yoga.

Metrics. Relatively few spirituality metrics included questions about personal religious and spiritual practices. These included spiritual interview tools, such as SPIRIT (Maugans, 1996) and scales, such as FACIT-Sp (Brady et al., 1999).

Well-being outcomes. Personal religious and spiritual practices are linked to improved health and functioning. Hackney and Sanders's (2003) meta-analysis found an overall effect of religiosity on mental health. In particular, they found highly significant correlations for "personal devotion"—that is, individual religious beliefs and practices— with mental health.

Religious and spiritual practices may take many forms, for example, meditation and mindfulness, prayer and other spiritual rituals, or attending religious activities. Each of these may have distinct effects on well-being. For instance, a review of clinical applications for meditation showed benefits for a number of clinical outcomes, such as decreased stress, as well as physical indicators of stress, and physical symptoms, such as immune functioning (Hart, 2007). Seeking to understand the practical applications of mindfulness, Brown and colleagues (2007) review evidence, obtained using various methodologies, demonstrating its benefits for mental health psychological well-being and physical health.

Moberg (2005) reviewed research showing that prayer had therapeutic value for anxiety and depression and led to improved recovery following surgery. Members of a religious youth group self-reported praise and worship activities as most important to their spiritual well-being and as fostering a sense of connection among them (Tshabalala and Patel, 2010).

Baldwin and colleagues (2008) suggest that veterans with higher reported spiritual quality of life may have benefited from companions who facilitate their participation in religious or spiritual activities. As an example of research within one particular religious group, one study found, using a cross-sectional survey of college students, that Mormons who actively attended church weekly reported better health status than less-active

21

Mormons, less-active non-Mormons, and people with no religious affiliation (Merrill and Salazar, 2002). However, a study of gender differences in depression in 2,989 Mormon adults ages 65 to 100 found that church attendance was associated with greater depression in men but less depression in women (Norton et al., 2008). It may therefore be important to consider how different dimensions of spiritual fitness may affect demographic subgroups differently.[9] "Spiritual symptoms" (i.e., poor spiritual fitness) have also been strongly associated, in a low-income, minority sample, with greater mental health and primary care use and lower reported health status (Katerndahl, 2008).

Religious practices and attendance in various forms also appear to be associated with decreased substance use. Wiist et al. (2010) conducted an online survey of over 1,200 Buddhists, finding that adherents follow generally similar health behaviors to the overall U.S. population, although a smaller proportion of Buddhists reported smoking. A survey of undergraduates found that family church attendance and parental religiosity acted as protective factors against adolescent substance use (Merrill, Folsom, and Christopherson, 2005). This relationship was particularly strong in Mormons, who in this survey were especially likely to report that substance use was inconsistent with their religious beliefs.

Resilience outcomes. Certain religious practices, such as meditation, influence resilience outcomes. A survey of Buddhists showed that time spent generally meditating (as opposed to time spent specifically in mindfulness meditation) was related to psychological mindfulness (Wiist et al., 2010), which may positively influence overall health. In a random trial involving college students, spiritual meditation had a stronger effect than did secular meditation on pain tolerance and mood, anxiety, and spiritual health (Wachholtz and Pargament, 2005). Individual spiritual meditation, performed daily for one month, showed similar advantages of secular meditation on decreasing migraine headaches, which are often associated with depression and anxiety, in addition to increasing pain tolerance, well-being, and daily spiritual experiences (Wachholtz and Pargament, 2008). Meditation focused on fostering compassion (a typical core spiritual value) reduced some physiological and behavioral stress response in a randomized, controlled trial (Pace et al., 2009), although more research needs to be done to determine its effects on "stress reactivity." A randomized controlled study of transcendental meditation showed that college student participants who learned its techniques appeared to be buffered from stress (i.e., during finals week) in several ways, including improved brain functioning and decreased tiredness (Travis et al., 2009). Finally, in an uncontrolled pilot study, Iraq and Afghanistan veterans with combat-related post-traumatic stress

---

[9] The literature on spirituality interventions, discussed below, also suggests the importance of accounting for demographic diversity.

disorder (PTSD) were trained in transcendental meditation techniques, which they then practiced daily for 12 weeks (Rosenthal et al., 2011). The veterans showed improvements in PTSD symptoms and quality-of-life measures, although these measures were not compared against a control group.

Support from a Spiritual Community

Support from a spiritual community, religious or otherwise, constitutes the social aspects of spiritual fitness. This construct includes, for example, how active people are in their spiritual community and the extent to which support is available (Koenig, 2002; LaRocca-Pitts, 2009; Pargament et al., 1998). Support from a spiritual or religious community is stronger among those with a religious affiliation than among those without such affiliation (Holland et al., 1998). As an example from within the military community, guard and reserve families cited religious organizations and churches as a particularly important source of community support during service member deployments (Werber et al., 2008). In particular, more "mature" spouses, as indicated by greater age, length of marriage, and higher spousal paygrade, were more likely to mention religious organizations as a resource.[10]

Metrics. As with the construct of personal religious and spiritual practices, comparatively few spirituality metrics included questions about spiritual support. The SBI-15R is one example of such a metric and explicitly includes social support derived from a spiritual or religious community as one of its subscales (Holland et al., 1998). Also of note is the Perceived Support from God Scale, which was developed for and validated with Christian African Americans, who commonly conceive of personal relationships with God (Hamilton et al., 2010). Although its two subscales, "support from God" and "meaning through a divine purpose," fit well with this construct and a spiritual worldview, respectively, the items refer only to a single God and do not account for other types of spiritual beliefs.

Well-being outcomes. Hackney and Sanders's (2003) meta-analysis found a strongly positive relationship between "institutional religion," or the "social and behavioral aspects of religion," such as attending religious services or participating in church activities, and mental health. Converging, albeit indirect, evidence appears to suggest that support from a spiritual community is generally beneficial to health and well-being. However, this work typically explores aspects of spiritual behavior that are only suggestive of spiritual support. For instance, a survey of male veterans who had had

---

[10] The role of a spiritual or religious community is discussed further in the companion report on the social fitness domain (McGene, 2013).

invasive surgical procedures showed that those with higher self-reported spiritual quality of life were more likely to have a wife or partner (Baldwin et al., 2008). The authors suggested that this companionship may have provided social support as well as facilitated religious or spiritual practices. Similarly, research linking church attendance to health status (e.g., Merrill and Salazar, 2002), in addition to illustrating the benefits of personal spiritual practices, also suggests the protective nature of spiritual support. Norton and colleagues (2008) point out that the inverse relationship between church attendance and depression may be due to several spiritual fitness constructs: increased purpose in life, social support, or that church attendance encourages personal spiritual practices. African American churches offer services, such as youth programs, that may provide social support (Boyd-Franklin, 2010). Paranjape and Kaslow (2010), conducting a cross-sectional observational study, found that both social support and spirituality (measured using the SWBS) were independently associated with better mental health among older African American women. However, this study did not explore the interactions between social support, spirituality, and health.

Resilience outcomes. Social support from a spiritual community appears to provide people, such those with existing difficulties, with coping resources. A literature review of spirituality in people with chronic illness suggests that connectedness with others (e.g., transcendence) within a spiritual community can lead to opportunities for more concrete, broader social support than that limited just to that spiritual community (Nichols and Hunt, 2011). These connections can help people with chronic illness by affecting positive adjustment and adaptation. Another example of beneficial spiritual support suggests that the effects of church-based social support may outweigh those of secular support. A cross-sectional survey of 548 Christian churchgoers (over age 66) found that spiritual support helped them cope with stress from financial difficulties (as measured by change in self-reported health), whereas secular support did not produce this protective effect (Krause, 2006). However, Krause notes that the survey design (i.e., from a single point in time) also makes it possible that the causal relationship between self-reported health and stress from financial difficulties could have been reversed. Earlier research by Krause and his colleagues (2001) on a nationwide sample of Presbyterians suggested that such spiritual support benefits may accrue by making people more likely to use religious coping methods (e.g., to look for a spiritually based lesson to be learned from a problem). However, the reliance on Christian, and in particular, Presbyterian, participants may limit the generalizability of Krause and colleagues' findings on spiritual versus secular support.

Spiritual Coping

Spiritual coping refers to the extent to which individuals use their beliefs as a source of comfort to deal with stress and strain (e.g., Brady et al., 1999; Borneman, Ferrell, and Puchalski, 2010; Pargament et al., 1998). The comfort derived from spiritual or religious beliefs may stem from optimism and hope (especially in a Western religious worldview) and a sense of meaning and purpose in life (Koenig, 2002). According to Pargament and colleagues (1998), positive religious coping includes, for example, "seeking spiritual support, religious forgiveness, collaborative religious coping, benevolent religious reappraisal." Negative religious coping includes "spiritual discontent, reappraisals of punishment from God and demonic involvement, and of God's powers, and interpersonal religious discontent." Although much of the relevant literature we identified referred specifically to "religious coping," e.g., Pargament et al., 1998), some studies specifically distinguished or made sure to talk about "spiritual coping" (e.g., Wachholtz, Pearce, and Koenig, 2007).

Metrics. As with the other spiritual fitness constructs, several metrics included questions about how the comfort provided by spiritual beliefs or distress caused by those beliefs (e.g., CSI-MEMO; Koenig, 2002). There is also a widely used measure that focuses on religious coping, the rCOPE (Pargament et al., 1998). This scale distinguishes between positive and negative patterns of coping and contains both items that refer to spirituality in general and to God specifically.

Well-being outcomes. Spiritual coping appears to have mixed effects on well-being outcomes. In part, this may be because there are different types of spiritual coping (e.g., with or without the role of a personalized agent such as God), which may have different effects on well-being (e.g., anxiety; Pargament, 2007). A meta-analysis of studies about religion and coping with stress found a positive relationship between religious coping and psychological adjustment to stress, and included several positive well-being outcomes (Ano and Vasconcelles, 2005). Using the rCOPE scale, Pargament and colleagues (1998) found that positive religious coping was associated with better psychological and spiritual outcomes and negative religious coping with worse outcomes. Poorer physical health (including PTSD) was inversely associated with the use of religious coping, both positive and negative. Negative religious coping, or religious struggle, is also associated with greater mortality in elderly ill individuals, as described in a longitudinal cohort study by Pargament and colleagues (2001). In ill patients, religious struggle may include anger with God, feeling punished by God, and believing that the devil is at work in the illness.

Trauma survivors may use spiritual coping for post-traumatic stress. Notably, evidence suggests that more generally spiritual coping (e.g., related to purpose in life) drives post-traumatic growth[11] and improved well-being, as opposed to coping that is more narrowly religious. Individuals with traumatic symptoms may be motivated to attempt greater use of religious coping strategies (Pargament et al., 1998). Harris and colleagues (2008) interviewed Christian church members who had experienced a variety of traumas, including natural disasters, motor vehicle accidents, violent or sexual assault, and war or combat. In these self-identified trauma survivors, positive religious coping was related to post-traumatic growth, whereas religious struggle was associated with post-traumatic symptoms.[12] However, although these findings nominally involved *religious* coping only, the actual coping strategies reflected spiritual coping more generally. Other studies suggest that the spiritual worldview construct—that is, reflecting perspective-taking of meaning and purpose in life—is in fact most influential after trauma. Kennedy and colleagues (2000) examined changes in the role of spirituality and well-being following violent trauma. The majority (60 percent) of a sample of predominantly minority, female victims of sexual assault indicated greater spirituality (i.e., purpose in life) after the incident. The women in this group had slightly (but nonsignificant) increased well-being, and women who did not indicate greater spirituality reported significantly reduced well-being. Matheis, Tulsky, and Matheis (2006) explored quality of life and spirituality in individuals with spinal cord injuries, which often severely impair function and thus social and career opportunities. Interviewing 75 individuals (mostly Caucasian single men), they found that "existential spirituality," related to seeking purpose in life and measured using the SWBS, was associated with higher quality of life. In contrast, spiritual coping that was strictly religious was unrelated to quality of life.

Although spiritual coping has been positively associated with certain mental health outcomes, it may not necessarily be effective in coping with physical stressors, such as pain. For example, religious-based coping is not always protective for chronically ill individuals or those who suffer from extreme pain (e.g., arthritis). Ill patients consider religious and spiritual thoughts as coping resources, but a multisite cross-sectional study showed that they are weakly or not associated with adaptive coping with illness and pain

---

[11] Post-traumatic growth refers to positive outcomes experienced after trauma. Such outcomes are conceptualized separately and measured as distinct from PTSD (e.g., Tedeschi and Calhoun, 1996).

[12] In both cited studies (Harris et al., 2008; Pargament et al., 1998), post-traumatic growth and symptoms of post-traumatic stress were measured using different metrics, reflecting that people can experience both positive as well as negative outcomes following trauma.

(Büssing et al., 2009). Yet the sheer prevalence of religiosity and spirituality among ill people suggests that these are thought of as "significant sources of support."

Wachholtz and colleagues (2007) posit several pathways for how religious and spiritual coping may attenuate pain. One such explanation, equating pain with daily stressors and hassles, holds that religious coping and rituals can distract from these immediate stressors, freeing the mind "to integrate a more spiritual dimension into the individual's life." Another model involves psychosocial influences on mood and emotion, which influence pain perception. Wiech and colleagues (2009) argue that "some religious believers can modulate their experience of pain and that such analgesic effects might be based on cognitive reappraisal of the negative emotional impact of pain."

Resilience outcomes. Spiritual coping may influence psychological states that buffer stress, such as helping people cope with an uncertain world. For instance, belief in God has been experimentally shown to vary as perceived personal control is manipulated (Kay et al., 2009), suggesting that religious beliefs may help preserve people's sense of personal control. There is initial evidence that perceived control may to some degree underlie spirituality and well-being. Gauthier (2001), in her master's thesis, reports the results of a study showing that spirituality was marginally correlated with perceived control related to health activities and was more strongly correlated with positive health-promoting behaviors. Coping due to spiritual well-being (measured using the SWBS) mediated the relationship between multiple sclerosis patients' perceived uncertainty about illness and psychological adjustment to illness, albeit on a fairly homogeneous sample (McNulty, Livneh, and Wilson, 2004).

Mabe and Josephson (2004) suggest that, in children, the efficacy of religious coping may depend on an interaction with spiritual beliefs and the extent to which the child feels personal control over the stressful situation. For instance, children who believe in an all-powerful and benevolent God may cope better with stressors they perceive to be out of their control. Windham, Hooper, and Hudson (2005) also argue that religious and spiritual beliefs, involvement, and practices should have protective effects against child or adolescent school violence by providing a sense of purpose and identity formation as a buffer against feelings of emptiness and lack of meaning.

Evidence Suggests That Spiritual Fitness May Protect Against Suicide, Although Not in All Situations

The relationship between spirituality, religion, and suicide may be of particular interest to the military. With some exceptions, most evidence points to the protective role of spirituality and religion. Reviewing studies of spirituality and suicide since 2000, Koenig, King, and Carson (2012) found that 47 out of 70 relevant quantitative studies found "less positive attitudes toward suicide, fewer suicide attempts, and fewer completed suicides." Koenig and colleagues hypothesize that spirituality may protect against suicide indirectly, such as by preventing "the psychological, social, behavioral, and physical factors that drive people to commit suicide," or by influencing "genetic risk factors for suicide."

Several constructs of spiritual fitness may be linked to suicidality, such as religious affiliation. Moral objections to suicide and social connections promoted through religion (e.g., responsibility to family) appear to be protective factors against suicidal acts among depressed inpatients who were asked about their religious affiliation and social networks (Dervic et al., 2004). An analysis of a large-scale Canadian health survey examined the relationships between spiritual attitudes, religious affiliation, and suicidality (Rasic et al., 2009). Social support appeared to generally underlie various relationships between spirituality, religiosity, and suicidality (e.g., suicidal ideation), but religious attendance was associated with decreased suicide attempts even after controlling for social support. Koenig (2009) also mentions other potentially protective factors related to religion and spiritual fitness, such as religious coping and deriving a sense of meaning from religious beliefs.

Although most studies find that spirituality and religion are associated with decreased suicidality, evidence also exists to the contrary. In Koenig and colleagues' (2012) review, 23 of the 70 studies found either no relationship, mixed effects, or increased suicidality associated with spirituality. Some of these studies, Koenig and colleagues noted, have methodological or other issues that limit the generalizability of their results. Dervic and colleagues (2004) also note that stigma related to religious or moral objections to suicide may result in the underreporting of suicide or suicide attempts, precluding an actual association between moral objection to suicide and suicide attempts. Spirituality or religiosity may lead to increased suicide in certain situations or for specific reasons. As examples of these, Koenig and colleagues (2012) mention, respectively, suicide attacks or religious guilt as a result of committing some crime or perceived moral wrong.

A better understanding of spiritual and religious influences on suicidality may result in interventions that can address this important concern without unintended negative consequences. For instance, early interventions that precede suicidal thoughts or attempts may be able to overcome psychological, behavioral, or social problems known to be associated with suicidality (see Koenig, King, and Carson, 2012).

3. Interventions to Promote Spiritual Fitness

What can be done to enhance spiritual fitness? Various existing interventions (e.g., programs, counseling, or therapy) attempt to bolster spirituality, including some of its key constructs. To explore how the Air Force might improve spiritual fitness across the force, we sought out examples of religious or spiritual interventions that influenced these key factors for resilience and well-being. Specifically, we began by searching for (1) interventions that used the most widely adopted spiritual fitness metrics (e.g., the SWBS) and (2) empirical evidence of these interventions' efficacy.

Our search uncovered numerous efforts to bolster spirituality and encourage spiritual growth, although far fewer of these programs had been rigorously examined to determine their efficacy. Among the studies we found, we noted key constructs that interventions focused on, how interventions could be implemented, and the importance of diversity.

Spirituality-related interventions appeared to focus mainly on three constructs: (1) fostering a spiritual worldview and a sense of meaning, purpose, or transcendence, (2) strengthening spiritual coping abilities and (3) supporting spiritual and religious practices.

In particular, many of the interventions and empirical evidence we found were programs that, paralleling the abundance of academic inquiry regarding the transcendent spiritual worldview, focused on providing a sense of purpose in life. Providing purpose in life may also be as simple as affording the opportunity to care for others, such as taking care of another living being. Research on human-animal interaction suggests that providing prisoners with opportunity to raise service dogs gave them a renewed sense of purpose in life (Suthers-McCabe, Van Voorhees, and Fournier, 2004). Other ways may involve discussion or training and education in spiritual topics. For instance, Tuck and colleagues (2006) investigated the acceptability and feasibility of a six-week, support group–based, spiritual growth intervention intended to relieve stress. Partly by facilitating the search for meaning, this spiritual development program appeared to bolster stress-coping responses. Specifically, this descriptive longitudinal study found a significant decline in perceived stress and increased growth in spiritual perspective at a six-week follow-up, albeit with only 27 participants.

Spiritual Interventions Generally Focus on Individuals; Fewer Interventions Address the Unit, Family, and Community Levels

Institutions may implement spiritual interventions in a targeted manner. These interventions may be categorized accordingly, based on the level at which research addressed their influence on resilience factors: (1) individual, (2) unit, (3) family, and (4) community. Most such interventions focused on individuals; few programs were designed and implemented at the other levels of analysis.

Individual-level interventions could include spiritual practices, such as meditation and prayer, but also targeted delivery of services, such as counseling or therapy. Examples of unit-level interventions included using spirituality to bolster leadership. Family-level interventions included programs to support the spiritual needs of entire families or of family members of those in need. Finally, community-level interventions could seek to improve the spiritual fitness of specific portions of the population or to improve care providers' effectiveness.

Individual-Level Interventions

A number of individual-level spiritual fitness programs have been directed toward specific populations, often with good results. Children of military families, who may be vulnerable to anxiety and other adverse outcomes resulting from such stressors as parental deployment (Richardson et al., 2011), may also benefit from targeted interventions. These programs could draw from existing programs that target similarly at-risk youths, some of which have been have been empirically tested. Several such programs have been shown to be effective. For example, a review of 11 faith-based programs for homeless youth (Ferguson et al., 2007), based on surveys and follow-up interviews with 33 staff members and participants, found several commonalities among effective programs, such as using faith to instill hope, facilitating religious activities, and teaching spiritual values (e.g., integrity, empathy). In these programs, the 11 participating youth reported better health and feeling more positive and exhibited more positive behaviors and attitudes. From these results, the authors proposed that counselors and leaders, for example, can use individuals' faiths—whatever they might be—as a way to build hope and optimism. These spiritual resources, in turn, can lead to improved well-being outcomes. However, the results of this study may have limited generalizability beyond homeless youth. Kelley (2003) provides empirical evidence for how community empowerment and school-based programs improved youths' sense of community and direction in life. The programs in this study were based on "health realization"—a set of positive psychology-based principles, for example, viewing the mind as "a spiritual truth . . . that grounds the observable"—that are intended to promote well-being and resilience in youth. Another intervention for children and adolescents is described in RAND's evaluation of the Spirituality for Kids Program (Maestas and Gaillot, 2010). This after-school program, which was not religious,[13] was based on best practices in resilience literature and sought to "build four areas of personal strength: social competence, problem solving, autonomy and self-efficacy, and sense of purpose" (Maestas and Gaillot, 2010, p. 3). A randomized, controlled study used a validated survey instrument to measure children's positive behaviors (e.g., social skills) and negative behaviors (e.g., anxiety, depression) immediately after the intervention as well as 12 weeks later. Results showed that the program significantly increased children's positive behaviors and, to a slightly lesser extent, decreased negative behaviors.

Research on interventions for young adults, still in their formative years, may be useful for junior military officers as well as for family members of a similar age. One generalized spiritual education intervention, called "Winding Road," involved facilitated group discussion to help college undergraduates understand their spiritual struggles as part of a larger spiritual journey (Gear, Krumrei, and Pargament, 2009). Qualitative self-report data showed that these students experienced less spirituality-related and general distress and reported behaving more consistently with their personal values. Schooling at universities and colleges may inherently benefit young adults as well. After reviewing the results of a nation-wide survey of spirituality in college students (Astin et al., 2004), Astin and colleagues (2010) suggested that fundamental college experiences, such as civic engagement and exposure to diverse people and ideas, "contribute to students' spiritual growth." Also, growth in particular spiritual areas was also associated with satisfaction with various aspects of college (i.e., the institution).

In addition to formal programs and training, institutions can provide opportunities for individual spiritual practices and beliefs. An article describing a web-based survey of Buddhists noted the existence—but did not examine the impact—of online services that send out daily inspirational messages, which individuals can sign up to receive (Wiist et al., 2010). A number of more individually based spiritual practices have also been shown to benefit well-being and resilience, including prayer and meditation. For example, Moberg (2005) reviewed research showing that prayer had therapeutic value for anxiety and depression and led to improved recovery following surgery.

Studies of mindfulness and meditation techniques suggest possible ways that they may be employed to improve well-being. The various forms and techniques of meditation range fairly widely, as does evidence for their clinical and therapeutic effectiveness.

---

[13] The name of the program was subsequently changed to "Success for Kids" to reflect adjusted curriculum and appropriateness for use in public schools (Nicole Maestas, personal communication, April 2011).

These forms include mindful meditation (based on Buddhist philosophy), transcendental meditation (based on Hindu methods), and others (see Lindberg, 2005, for a review). A great deal of advice is anecdotal and based primarily on personal clinical or therapeutic experiences with meditation. For example, Hart (2007) discusses, from her own clinical standpoint, how interested patients could begin meditation therapy. There is also more empirical evidence regarding mindfulness and meditation. Lindberg (2005) reviews evidence on spirituality and meditation that is related to the health of the elderly. Elderly people can learn techniques that are effective in promoting spirituality along with psychological well-being. The extent to which these findings are generalizable to other socially isolated people may suggest ways in which meditation practices may be useful. For example, they may be helpful for military family members, who may find themselves with limited social capital because of frequent relocations (Harrell et al., 2004).

Mindfulness is a specific technique for directing attention, generally derived from Eastern philosophies, which may help well-being and increase a sense of the transcendent. Ekman et al. (2005) point out that, although Western psychological research and methods have typically focused on treating discernible problems, Buddhism teachings emphasize a notion of well-being that includes recognition of the interconnectedness of life. Training practices from Buddhism, such as mindfulness, may therefore profitably inform development of interventions for overall well-being and transcendence. Mindfulness as an intervention is suggested to help interrupt patterns of avoidant behavior relating to traumatic experiences and emotions. Follette and colleagues (2006) theorize that mindfulness can therefore also complement exposure therapies by giving traumatized persons the ability to "contact" the exposure stimuli to a greater extent than would be possible in vivo. The basis of these compassion-based treatments may be that self-compassion is inversely related to some symptoms of post-traumatic stress (Thompson and Waltz, 2008). Accordingly, Berceli and Napoli (2006) have proposed a mindfulness-based trauma prevention program for social workers and professional caregivers, either individually or in groups. In addition to the proposed prevention programs, post-trauma treatments have been developed, such as two treatments for traumatized children (Catani et al., 2009): a narrative-based therapy and a treatment emphasizing meditation and relaxation. Although ethical concerns precluded a third (i.e., control) group, recovery rates in both treatment conditions were greater than untreated recovery rates in other populations of traumatized children.

In addition to their effects on traumatic stress, mindfulness techniques may also help to reduce stress in general. Mindfulness meditation therapy reduced anxiety and depression in Japanese cancer patients (Ando et al., 2009). However, this study had a small sample and did not use a control group, limiting the extent to which strong conclusions may be drawn regarding the effectiveness of this therapy. Shapiro and colleagues (2008) tested the effectiveness of two spiritually based interventions—an "explicitly mindfulness-based program" and a passage meditation-based program (Shapiro et al., 2008). College undergraduates randomly assigned to receive either of these interventions demonstrated increased mindfulness (e.g., self-reported as paying increased attention to immediate experiences) at eight-week follow-ups. These increases in mindfulness mediated decreases in stress and rumination.

The principles of mindfulness have also been successfully applied as part of dialectical behavior therapy (DBT). Mindfulness in DBT was derived both from Zen Buddhist and Christian contemplative practices and involves being aware of and "unified with" one's current experiences, aiming to achieve a balance between emotional and rational thought processes, as well as between attempting to change or accept problematic thoughts and behaviors (see Lynch et al., 2006; Robins, 2002). DBT has been well validated in several randomized clinical trials as effective for treating clinical conditions (e.g., depression, borderline personality disorder) and suicidality (e.g., suicide attempts and suicidal ideation; Lynch et al., 2006) and has been adapted for various clinical settings (Robins and Chapman, 2004). Mindfulness in DBT is theorized to be useful by, for example, redirecting attention away from worrying events (Lynch et al., 2006; Robins and Chapman, 2004).

Unit-Level Interventions

Spiritual leadership has been shown to affect military unit performance, a relationship mediated by these constructs of spiritual well-being (Fry et al., 2011). A survey of organizational commitment and productivity, along with measures of spiritual leadership and well-being (adapted for military use), was administered to cadets at the United States Military Academy. The cadets' scores were compared against performance ratings, aggregated for a squad level of analysis. Spiritual leadership was positively associated with organizational commitment and several performance measures. Fry and colleagues propose that units who have hope and faith in the organization's vision and who experience a sense of calling and purpose will be more motivated and productive. For the military, this may mean greater commitment to the "warrior ethos" of putting the mission first and valuing camaraderie.

Effective unit-level leadership may thus be able to overcome certain barriers to bolstering spiritual fitness that care providers and spiritual counselors face. For instance, the concept of spiritual leadership may be a useful model for how leaders might be effective. Spiritual leadership (e.g., Fry, 2009) calls for a leader to possess an inner spirituality that allows that leader to facilitate in others two key spiritual fitness constructs: (1) self-transcendence to serve others) and (2) establishment of a mutually supportive culture and sense of community. Qualitatively examining ten well-known human rights leaders in depth, including exploring specific events in their lives, Parameshwar (2005) concluded that a key achievement by these leaders was to subordinate their personal goals and motives in the service of a higher purpose (i.e., self-transcendence) that inspired their followers to behaviors and actions. Moskos and Wood (1988) similarly emphasize service to others as well as to community, stating that military leaders must "affirm altruistic norms at the micro or small-unit level."

Family-Level Interventions

Enhancing spirituality in care providers may improve care and family members' experiences. When a loved one requires medical treatment, family members may take comfort in being present as much as possible. A correlational survey showed that health care professionals who are more spiritual are also more likely to perceive the value of holistic care and to see the presence of family members as beneficial to patients as well as a right (Baumhover and Hughes, 2009).

Military chaplains may face complicating issues, such as untreated mental health problems, when promoting spiritual fitness at the family level. For example, one Navy chaplain, writing about family issues in time of war, claims that many chaplains who do not have mental health or counseling training are nevertheless called upon to perform those duties, for which they are likely unprepared (Howard and Cox, 2007). Chaplains, Howard and Cox caution, should stay within their areas of expertise (e.g., pastoral or spiritual issues) while maintaining the ability to provide moral guidance and help people of all faiths, or of none. The primary function for chaplains, in this view, in addition to the obvious role of supporting each family's particular moral and spiritual beliefs or chosen religious practices, is in more generally helping clients increase coping skills and resilience.

Community-Level Interventions

Community-level interventions could include programs targeted at specific populations and support for leaders and care providers. First, spiritual educational programs—such as morality and ethics courses—may be effective in development of personal values and morals. Verweij and colleagues (2007) conducted a study of moral knowledge that compared 400 Dutch officers, officer candidates, and university students. They found generally high moral awareness in the military populations, which had typically undergone ethics training. These military members' knowledge of specific ethics models and codes of conduct further suggested the effect of their military ethics training. Therefore, to the extent that ethics education is comparable in the Air Force and in other militaries, these results suggest that this type of education or schooling is effective for teaching moral values.

Regardless of whom they target, programs intended to serve the community can only be as effective as the people who implement those programs. Thus, those who directly influence an overall community will be the people who provide care and leadership to Airmen and their families. This is true, in particular, for health care providers. First, according to one researcher, improving health care providers' ability to "provide spiritual care" can enhance total fitness by improving treatment of mental and physical health (Lewallen, 2009). Second, increased use of spiritual assessments as a routine component of health services may serve to emphasize the importance of spiritual fitness. Indeed, Nichols and Hunt (2011) suggest that using spiritual assessments in clinical care may help reinforce the legitimacy of spiritual fitness in "the counseling discussion and process" of treatment.

However, health care providers face certain barriers in providing effective spiritual care. Tanyi (2002) offers several examples relating to nurses, including lack of time, training, and privacy to counsel patients. She suggests that overcoming these barriers, by allowing nurses to better understand patients' spiritual values, will "enhance optimal holistic health care." Lewallen (2009) similarly argues that nurses should be trained to perform spiritual assessments independently of their own or the patients' religious or spiritual beliefs, again to improve holistic care across medical settings. And although many spiritual assessments tools emphasize end-of-life care, Lewallen argues that spiritual assessments and care are equally important in other situations, such as for childbirth. A self-study program intended to teach nurses how to discuss spirituality with patients was indeed found to be effective for nursing students as well as practicing registered nurses in increasing skill and knowledge in empathetic spiritual care communication (Taylor et al., 2008). The course material consisted of, for example, creating verbal response strategies to patients' expression of spiritual pain. 201 nursing students and registered nurses participated in a study of this program, completing pre- and post-test measures of their attitudes toward spiritual caregiving and their ability to respond empathetically. After having completed this material, participants' skills and ability to respond empathetically improved for both of these groups. Another training program, the Eight-Point Programme (EPP), is designed to impart in health professionals the concept of "compassionate love" (Oman, Thoresen, and Hedberg, 2010). Caring for the well-being of others is the central concept of compassionate love, similar to the transcendent spiritual worldview. EPP is based on passage meditation, which draws inspiration from major spiritual traditions and is intended to be used by any spiritual tradition, or outside them. A randomized trial of health professionals with patient contact indicated that EPP was effective, even in a follow-up several months after the program, in reducing stress, but also in increasing compassionate love and related caregiving skills, such as empathy and forgiveness.

Social work literature also recognizes the importance of spirituality in providing holistic care to clients. Incorporating spirituality may allow social workers to address cultural diversity and apply techniques of meditation, relaxation, and contemplation (Carrington, 2010). Noting that social work is about teaching and developing individuals and community, Rothman (2009) suggests that social workers acquire greater knowledge of spirituality, acquire skills in using spiritual assessment tools, and, finally, work on self-awareness and personal growth. Dimidjian and Linehan (2003) have suggested that clinicians—even if they do not directly teach spiritual techniques—adopt mindfulness principles in their interactions with patients (e.g., nonjudgment, exhibiting compassion), which may provide a useful model of adaptive behavior.

Diversity of Religious and Spiritual Beliefs Suggests That Resilience Efforts Should Consider Culturally Appropriate Interventions

Because religious and spiritual practices and beliefs are diverse and often individual-specific, spirituality interventions need to be culturally appropriate to be inclusive. Therefore, a critical factor in considering how to improve spiritual fitness is cultural appropriateness and competence—that is, recognizing the diversity of beliefs and accordingly designing efforts to promote resilience. In other words, these efforts must be sensitive to cultural differences that may affect their influence on spiritual fitness. The significance of cultural appropriateness not only stems from DoD's responsibility to not promote any religion or set of beliefs over another but also was apparent from the literature we reviewed. For example, Rothman (2009) used the results of informal interviews about spirituality to suggest that a greater understanding of how spiritual experiences differ can allow health and service providers to better relate to clients and their experiences.

Spiritual diversity may affect interventions in several ways. First, spiritual diversity may occur within people of various race/ethnicity, religious traditions, or with no religion. Differences in spiritual beliefs across any of these groups, such as diverging notions of what is moral or of ideal behavior, may lead to different influences of spirituality on well-being. For instance, experimental studies have shown that Buddhist and Christian ideas of happiness and well-being differ (Tsai and Seppala, 2007). The effectiveness of efforts aimed at well-being and resilience should therefore differ between individuals of different spiritual beliefs, implying the need to carefully consider which ones a particular intervention will target. As with religious traditions, it is also important to not simply lump together all nonreligious individuals, who differ in beliefs as well as behaviors (Hwang, Hammer, and Cragun, 2009). This suggests that there cannot be a single set of interventions or programs for all of these "secular minorities."

One must also consider diversity not just of spiritual beliefs, but between population groups. For example, the relationship between religiousness and mental health differs by race/ethnicity (Cokley et al., 2010). Spirituality interventions may therefore benefit by targeting specific groups. At the community level, counseling or therapeutic providers can reach out to and involve African American churches, which typically play a major role in African American spirituality (Boyd-Franklin, 2010). Providers can do so by asking clients, colleagues, or contacts to facilitate these relationships, after which these churches might be effective bases for mental health interventions or services after such traumas as violence or disaster. Empirical research focusing on specific racial/ethnic groups provides some support for individual-level benefits, which may vary by group. Arnette and colleagues (2007) assessed therapeutic mental health interventions (e.g., weekly support groups) for traumatized (i.e., abused and suicidal) African American women. The authors interpreted the results (measured using the rCOPE and SWBS) of the intervention's efficacy as suggesting that culturally competent interventions should seek to understand clients' specific spiritual beliefs and how those inform the coping strategies that are chosen. However, others have suggested that specific knowledge of clients' spiritual or religious beliefs are unnecessary so long as counselors or care providers have a basic understanding of the clients' cultural values and are cautious to not impose their own beliefs (Boyd-Franklin, 2010). Finally, although there is evidence that interventions targeted directly at a high-risk Hispanic community can be effective in increasing spiritual well-being (Guinn and Vincent, 2002), the results do not specifically suggest that they are any more effective than are more general spiritual interventions.

4. Concluding Thoughts

After reviewing research on spirituality and religion, we identified key factors that appear to influence resilience and well-being. We investigated general relationships between spiritual fitness constructs and outcomes related to resilience and well-being. Spiritual fitness may influence resilience and well-being outcomes either directly, or indirectly by buffering stress. Finally, we explored interventions designed to address these spirituality constructs at various levels.

Spirituality appears to be largely beneficial for well-being. Koenig and colleagues (2012) reviewed 102 studies in 2000, 81 of which found positive associations between spirituality and well-being. Since that review, they found an additional 224 studies, 175 of which found positive associations between spirituality and well-being. Our findings regarding key constructs of spiritual fitness—spiritual worldview, personal religious or spiritual practices and rituals, support from spiritual and religious communities, and spiritual coping—largely echo these overall findings. We identified research linking each of these spiritual fitness constructs to improved resilience and well-being outcomes.

These findings suggest that resilience and well-being interventions may benefit from addressing people's spiritual needs. Pargament (2007) has argued that spiritual beliefs are central to many people's concerns, and, as such, spirituality must be integrated or accounted for in therapy. Such clinical support could draw on such spiritual resources as spiritual knowledge or wisdom (e.g., religious texts), experiences (e.g., prayer), relationships (e.g., religious leaders), or coping. Moberg (2005) also notes research showing the benefits of explicitly demonstrating attention to spiritual matters in clinical care.

Indeed, we found numerous examples of spiritual interventions that have been demonstrated to benefit resilience and well-being. These interventions primarily targeted individuals, but some also focused on families, military units, or communities. The spiritual interventions we reviewed also varied by type, including individual spiritual practices and rituals, therapy, counseling, or training programs. Finally, the studies evaluating these interventions often had very different research designs, ranging from observational correlational studies to those with fully randomized clinical trials. This research may inform current and planned Air Force efforts to enhance the spiritual fitness of its Airmen and family members.

Below we offer several recommendations regarding interventions or programs to bolster spiritual fitness and complement the existing efforts of Air Force chaplains and religious leaders in the communities surrounding Air Force bases. These recommendations are based on our review of spirituality research and should provide a foundation for broader recommendations to support the development of interventions or programs to promote resilience across the Air Force.[14]

Recommendation 1: Expand Support for Diverse Spiritual Needs Within the Air Force Community

The importance of cultural appropriateness was very apparent in this literature. Going forward, it will be important to understand how to ensure that the Air Force is supporting not only the needs of Airmen and families within the major religious traditions, but also individuals of other faiths as well as secular individuals. Recent efforts to support atheists' spiritual needs—by forming secular communities (e.g., Breen, 2011; Dao, 2011) and seeking official military recognition—suggest an unmet need. The use of both the terms "religious" and "spiritual" in training and outreach efforts may help avoid alienating populations who may otherwise feel excluded. Of note is that the Air Force has "Free Exercise of Religion" training, which does not appear to mention spirituality. Likewise, emphasizing generalized spiritual interventions that target pluralistic or nonreligious audiences, such as Winding Road (Gear, Krumrei, and Pargament, 2009), may also help support diverse needs within the Air Force community by supplementing already available religious services.

Recommendation 2: Leverage Existing Evidence-Based Guidance on Implementing Spiritual Interventions

Spiritual interventions may benefit from understanding best practices, potential pitfalls, or lessons learned from implementing similar interventions. For example, evidence-based guidance exists on how to implement spiritual interventions, such as a resource guide on the role of faith-based organizations in public safety (Hercik et al., 2005), commissioned by the National Institutes of Justice. This guide was specifically intended for policymakers "interested in identifying promising faith-based organizations and innovative faith-based interventions."

---

[14] The overarching report in this series (Meadows and Miller, forthcoming) provides further recommendations that encompass all the total fitness domains.

Recommendation 3: Explore Alternative Approaches to Enhancing Spiritual Fitness

Further research can likely inform the design of interventions to enhance spiritual fitness, especially regarding their influence on key resilience and well-being factors. Future studies may wish to explore how to better use mindfulness and meditation techniques, such as by blending interventions based on mainstream psychological theories with those based on Eastern traditions. Chambers and colleagues (2009), for example, have put forth a theory of "mindful emotion regulation" as an attempt to integrate the constructs of mindfulness and emotion regulation. New spirituality interventions could seek to draw from theoretical work such as this. Another possibility would be to use open-ended spiritual assessments, such as those currently used in clinical care, as opportunities to disclose traumatic emotions. Emotional disclosure—the process of verbally expressing traumatic thoughts and feelings—helps "meaning making" and can have profound effects on psychological as well as physical health (Harber and Pennebaker, 1992). In other words, Airmen and family members could be given greater opportunity to, or be encouraged to, express themselves verbally about traumatic experiences. By creating narratives around traumatic experiences, verbal expressions of emotions are thought to help individuals "make meaning" out of those traumas. Institutional policies might be modified or implemented that provide for such time and opportunity. These policies could be supplemented by directly encouraging leaders at the unit level to do so.

Recommendation 4: Consider Non-Spirituality-Specific Interventions

Intriguingly, even interventions that do not explicitly address any of the spiritual fitness constructs we identified may nevertheless enhance spiritual fitness. A multidimensional intervention that focused first on personal growth and then on "entrepreneurial" ability was administered to a high-risk Hispanic community (Guinn and Vincent, 2002). Although this intervention was culturally targeted, it did not directly address any of the key constructs of spiritual fitness. Yet it still increased spiritual well-being, as measured by the SWBS. (However, note that although these findings were based on randomized samples of this population, pre-test measures were not available, meaning that only post-intervention comparisons between groups were obtained.) This result suggests that there may be potential for promoting spiritual fitness that may not require only narrowly focused interventions and that targeting other areas may be indirectly beneficial.

Bibliography

Anandarajah, Gowri, and Ellen Hight, "Spirituality and Medical Practice: Using the Hope Questions as a Practical Tool for Spiritual Assessment," *American Family Physician,* Vol. 63, No. 1, January 1, 2001, pp. 81–88, 89.

Ando, Michiyo, Tatsuya Morita, Tatsuo Akechi, Sayoko Ito, Masaya Tanaka, Yuka Ifuku, and Toshimichi Nakayama, "The Efficacy of Mindfulness-Based Meditation Therapy on Anxiety, Depression, and Spirituality in Japanese Patients with Cancer," *Journal of Palliative Medicine,* Vol. 12, November 12, 2009, pp. 1091–1094.

Ano, Gene G., and Erin B. Vasconcelles, "Religious Coping and Psychological Adjustment to Stress: A Meta-Analysis," *Journal of Clinical Psychology,* Vol. 61, No. 4, April 2005, pp. 461–480.

Arnette, Natalie C., Nathan Mascaro, M. Carmen Santana, Shane Davis, and Nadine J. Kaslow, "Enhancing Spiritual Well-Being Among Suicidal African American Female Survivors of Intimate Partner Violence," *Journal of Clinical Psychology*, Vol. 63, No. 10, 2007, pp. 909–924.

Astin, Alexander W., Helen S. Astin, Alyssa N. Bryant, Shannon Calderone, Jennifer A. Lindholm, and Katalin Szelenyi, *The Spiritual Life of College Students: A National Study of College Students' Search for Meaning and Purpose*, Los Angeles: University of California, 2004.

Astin, Alexander W., Helen S. Astin, and Jennifer A. Lindholm, *Key Findings from the First National Longitudinal Study of Undergraduates' Spiritual Growth*, Los Angeles: University of California, 2010.

Baldwin, Carol M., Marcia Grant, Christopher Wendel, Susan Rawl, C. Max Schmidt, Clifford Ko, and Robert S. Krouse, "Influence of Intestinal Stoma on Spiritual Quality of Life of U.S. Veterans," *Journal of Holistic Nursing,* Vol. 26, No. 3, September 2008, pp. 185–194.

Baumhover, Nancy, and Linda Hughes, "Spirituality and Support for Family Presence During Invasive Procedures and Resuscitations in Adults," *American Journal of Critical Care,* Vol. 18, No. 4, July 2009, pp. 357–366.

Berceli, David, and Maria Napoli, "A Proposal for a Mindfulness-Based Trauma Prevention Program for Social Work Professionals," *Complementary Health Practice Review,* Vol. 11, No. 3, October 2006, pp. 153–165.

Borneman, Tami, Betty Ferrell, and Christina M. Puchalski, "Evaluation of the FICA Tool for Spiritual Assessment," *Journal of Pain and Symptom Management,* Vol. 40, No. 2, August 2010, pp. 163–173.

Boyd-Franklin, Nancy, "Incorporating Spirituality and Religion into the Treatment of African American Clients," *The Counseling Psychologist,* Vol. 38, No. 7, 2010, pp. 976–1000.

Brady, Marianne J., Amy H. Peterman, George Fitchett, May Mo, and David Cella, "A Case for Including Spirituality in Quality of Life Measurement in Oncology," *Pscho-Oncology,* Vol. 8, 1999, pp. 417–428.

Breen, Tom, "Army Group Says There Are Atheists in Foxholes," *Associated Press,* 2011.

Brown, Kirk W., Richard M. Ryan, and J. D. Creswell, "Mindfulness: Theoretical Foundations and Evidence for Its Salutary Effects," *Psychological Inquiry,* Vol. 18, No. 4, 2007, pp. 211–237.

Büssing, Arndt, Andreas Michalsen, Hans-Joachim Balzat, Ralf-Achim Grünther, Thomas Ostermann, Edmund A. M. Neugebauer, and Peter F. Matthiessen, "Are Spirituality and Religiosity Resources for Patients with Chronic Pain Conditions?" *Pain Medicine,* Vol. 10, November 2, 2009, pp. 327–339.

Carrington, Ann M., "Spiritual Paradigms: A Response to Concerns within Social Work in Relation to the Inclusion of Spirituality," *Journal of Religion and Spirituality in Social Work: Social Thought,* Vol. 29, No. 4, November 6, 2010, pp. 300–320.

Catani, Claudia, Mahendran Kohiladevy, Martina Ruf, Elisabeth Schauer, Thomas Elbert, and Frank Neuner, "Treating Children Traumatized by War and Tsunami: A Comparison Between Exposure Therapy and Meditation-Relaxation in North-East Sri Lanka," *BMC Psychiatry,* Vol. 9, No. 22, May 13, 2009, pp. 1–11.

Chambers, Richard, Eleonora Gullone, and Nicholas B. Allen, "Mindful Emotion Regulation: An Integrative Review," *Clinical Psychology Review,* Vol. 29, February 2009, pp. 560–572.

Cloninger, C. Robert, Dragan M. Svrakic, and Thomas R. Przybeck, "A Psychobiological Model of Temperament and Character," *Archives of General Psychiatry,* Vol. 50, December 1993, pp. 975–990.

Cokley, Kevin, Daniel Garcia, Brittany Hall-Clark, Kimberly Tran, and Azucena Rangel, "The Moderating Role of Ethnicity in the Relation Between Religiousness and Mental Health Among Ethnically Diverse College Students," *Journal of Religion and Health,* Vol. 51, No. 3, September 2010, pp. 890–907.

Danesh, H. B., "Creating a Culture of Healing in Multiethnic Communities: An Integrative Approach to Prevention and Amelioration of Violence-Induced Conditions," *Journal of Community Psychology,* Vol. 36, No. 6, 2008, pp. 814–832.

Dao, James, "Atheists Seek Chaplain Role in the Military," *New York Times*, April 26, 2011.

Defense Centers of Excellence for Psychological Health and Traumatic Brain Injury (DCoE), *Traumatic Brain Injury,* 2011. As of April 9, 2011: http://www.dcoe.health.mil/TraumaticBrainInjury.aspx

Dervic, Kanita, Maria Oquendo, Michael Grunebaum, Steve Ellis, and Ainsley K. Burke, "Religious Affiliation and Suicide Attempt," *Psychiatry,* Vol. 161, December 2004, pp. 2303–2308.

Dimidjian, Sona, and Marsha M. Linehan, "Defining an Agenda for Future Research on the Clinical Application of Mindfulness Practice," *Clinical Psychology: Science and Practice,* Vol. 10, No. 2, June 2003, pp. 166–171.

Ecklund, Elaine Howard, and Elizabeth Long, "Scientists and Spirituality," *Sociology of Religion*, Vol. 72, No. 3, 2011, pp. 253–274.

Ekman, Paul, Richard J. Davidson, Matthieu Ricard, and B. Alan Wallace, "Buddhist and Psychological Perspectives on Emotions and Well-Being," *Current Directions in Psychological Science,* Vol. 14, No. 2, 2005, pp. 59–63.

Elkins, David N., L. James Hedstrom, Lori L. Hughes, J. Andrew Leaf, and Cheryl Saunders, "Toward a Humanistic-Phenomenological Spirituality: Definition, Description, and Measurement," *Journal of Humanistic Psychology,* Vol. 28, No. 4, 1988, pp. 5–18.

Emmons, Robert A., *The Psychology of Ultimate Concerns: Motivation and Spirituality in Personality,* New York: The Guilford Press, 1999.

Faribors, Bagheri, Akbarizadeh Fatemeh, and Hatami Hamidreza, "The Relationship Between Nurses' Spiritual Intelligence and Happiness in Iran," *Procedia Social and Behavioral Sciences,* Vol. 5, 2010, pp. 1556–1561.

Ferguson, Kristin M., Wu Qiaobing, Grace Dyrness, and Donna Spruijt-Metz, "Perceptions of Faith and Outcomes in Faith-Based Programs for Homeless Youth," *Journal of Social Service Research,* Vol. 33, No. 4, 2007, pp. 25–43.

Ferrell, B. R., K. H. Dow, S. Leigh, J. Ly, and P. Gulasekaram, "Quality of Life in Long-Term Cancer Survivors," *Oncology Nursing Forum,* Vol. 22, No. 6, 1995, pp. 915–922.

Flórez, Karen R., Regina A. Shih, and Margret T. Martin, *Nutritional Fitness and Resilience: A Review of Relevant Constructs, Measures, and Links to Well-Being,* Santa Monica, Calif.: RAND Corporation, RR-105-AF, forthcoming.

Follette, Victoria, Kathleen Palm, and Adria Pearson, "Mindfulness and Trauma: Implications for Treatment," *Journal of Rational-Emotive & Cognitive-Behavior Therapy,* Vol. 24, No. 1, August 2, 2006, pp. 45–61.

Fry, Louis W. (Jody), "Spiritual Leadership as a Model for Student Inner Development," *Journal of Leadership Studies,* Vol. 3, No. 3, November 3, 2009, pp. 79–82.

Fry, Louis W., Sean T. Hannah, Michael Noel, and Fred O. Walumbwa, "Impact of Spiritual Leadership on Unit Performance," *The Leadership Quarterly*, Vol. 22, No. 2, 2011, pp. 259–270.

Gauthier, Janine E., *Spirituality, Health Locus of Control, and Wellness in Organizational Health Promotion and Wellness Programs*, master's thesis, Dallas: University of North Texas, 2001.

Gear, Maria R., Elizabeth J. Krumrei, and Kenneth I. Pargament, "Development of a Spiritually-Sensitive Intervention for College Students Experiencing Spiritual Struggles: Winding Road," *Journal of College & Character,* Vol. 10, No. 4, April 2009, pp. 1–5.

Graham, Jesse, Brian A. Nosek, Jonathan Haidt, Ravi Iyer, Spassena Koleva, and Peter H. Ditto, "Mapping the Moral Domain," *Journal of Personality and Social Psychology*, Vol. 101, No. 2, January 17, 2011, pp. 366–385.

Guinn, Bobby, and Vern Vincent, "A Health Intervention on Latina Spiritual Well-Being Constructs: An Evaluation," *Hispanic Journal of Behavioral Sciences,* Vol. 24, No. 3, August 2002, pp. 379–391.

Hackney, Charles H., and Glenn S. Sanders, "Religiosity and Mental Health: A Meta-Analysis of Recent Studies," *Journal for the Scientific Study of Religion,* Vol. 42, No. 1, March 2003, pp. 43–56.

Haidt, Jonathan, Silvia H. Koller, and Maria G. Dias, "Affect, Culture, and Morality, or Is It Wrong to Eat Your Dog?" *Attitudes and Social Cognition,* Vol. 65, No. 4, 1993, pp. 613–628.

Hamilton, Jill B., Jamie Crandell, J. Kameron Carter, and Mary Lynn, "Reliability and Validity of the Perspectives of Support from God Scale," *Nursing Research*, Vol. 59, 2010, pp. 102–109.

Harber, Kent D., and James W. Pennebaker, "Overcoming Traumatic Memories," in Sven-Ake Christianson, ed., *The Handbook of Emotion and Memory: Research and Theory*, Hillsdale, N.J.: Lawrence Erlbaum Associates, 1992 pp. 359–387.

Harrell, Margaret C., Nelson Lim, Laura Werber, and Daniela Golinelli, *Working Around the Military: Challenges to Military Spouse Employment and Education*, Santa Monica, Calif.: RAND Corporation, MG-196-OSD, 2004. As of June 22, 2012: http://www.rand.org/pubs/monographs/MG196.html

Harris, J. Irene, Christopher R. Erbes, Brian E. Engdahl, Raymond H. A. Olson, Ann Marie Winskowski, and Joelle McMahill, "Christian Religious Functioning and Trauma Outcomes," *Journal of Clinical Psychology,* Vol. 64, No. 1, 2008, pp. 17–29.

Hart, Jane, "Clinical Applications for Meditation: A Review and Recommendations," *Alternative and Complementary Therapies,* Vol. 14, No. 4, February 2007, pp. 24–29.

Hatch, Robert, Mary Ann Burg, Debra S. Naberhaus, and Linda K. Hellmich, "The Spiritual Involvement and Beliefs Scale: Development and Testing of a New Instrument," *The Journal of Family Practice,* Vol. 46, No. 6, June 1998, pp. 476–486.

Hercik, Jeanette, Richard Lewis, Bradley Myles, Caterina Gouvis, Janine Zweig, Alyssa Whitby, Gabriella Rico, and Elizabeth McBride, *Development of a Guide to Resources on Faith-Based Organizations in Criminal Justice*, Washington, D.C.: The Urban Institute, 2005.

Holland, Jimmie C., Kathryn M. Kash, Steven Passik, Melissa Gronert, Antonio Sison, Marguerite Lederberg, Simcha M. Russak, Lea Baider, and Bernard Fox, "A Brief Spiritual Beliefs Inventory for Use in Quality of Life Research in Life-Threatening Illness," *Psycho-Oncology,* Vol. 7, 1998, pp. 460–469.

Holt, Cheryl L., Emily Schulz, Lee Caplan, Victor Blake, Vivian L. Southward, and Ayanna V. Buckner, "Assessing the Role of Spirituality in Coping Among African Americans Diagnosed with Cancer," *Journal of Religion and Health*, Vol. 51, No. 2, 2011, pp. 507–521.

Hood, Ralph W., Jr., "The Construction and Preliminary Validation of a Measure of Reported Mystical Experience," *Journal for the Scientific Study of Religion*, Vol. 14, No. 1, March 1975, pp. 29–41.

Howard, Michael, and Ruth Cox, "Family Issues in Time of War: A Chaplain's Perspective," *Journal of the Association of Mormon Counselors and Psychotherapists,* Vol. 31, No. 1, 2007, pp. 55–69.

Hufford, David J., Matthew J. Fritts, and Jeffrey E. Rhodes, "Spiritual Fitness," in Wayne B. Jonas, Francis G. O'Connor, Patricia Deuster, and Christian Macedonia, eds., *Total Force Fitness for the 21st Century: A New Paradigm*, Supplement to *Military Medicine*, Vol. 175, No. 8, August 2010. As of June 21, 2012: http://www.siib.org/news/1099-SIIB/version/default/part/AttachmentData/data/ Total%20Force%20Fitness%20for%20the%2021st%20Century-- A%20New%20Paradigm.pdf

Hwang, Karen, Joseph H. Hammer, and Ryan T. Cragun, "Extending Religion-Health Research to Secular Minorities: Issues and Concerns," *Journal of Religion and Health*, Vol. 50, No. 3, 2009, pp. 608–622.

Jagers, Robert J., and Paula Smith, "Further Examination of the Spirituality Scale," *Journal of Black Psychology*, Vol. 22, No. 4, 1996, pp. 429–442.

Johnson, Douglas C., Melissa A. Polusny, Christopher R. Erbes, Daniel King, Lynda King, Brett T. Litz, Paula P. Schnurr, Matthew Friedman, Robert H. Pietrzak, and Steven M. Southwick, "Develement and Initial Validation of the Response to Stressful Experiences Scale," *Military Medicine*, Vol. 176, No. 2, February 2011, pp. 161–169.

Jonas, Wayne B., Francis G. O'Connor, Patricia Deuster, and Christian Macedonia, eds., *Total Force Fitness for the 21st Century: A New Paradigm*, Supplement to *Military Medicine*, Vol. 175, No. 8, August 2010. As of June 21, 2012: http://www.siib.org/news/1099-SIIB/version/default/part/AttachmentData/data/ Total%20Force%20Fitness%20for%20the%2021st%20Century--A%20New% 20Paradigm.pdf

Katerndahl, David A., "Impact of Spiritual Symptoms and Their Interactions on Health Services and Life Satisfaction," *Annals of Family Medicine*, Vol. 6, No. 5, September–October 2008, pp. 412–420.

Kay, Aaron C., Jennifer A. Whitson, Danielle Gaucher, and Adam D. Galinsky, "Compensatory Control: Achieving Order Through the Mind, Our Institutions, and the Heavens," *Current Directions in Psychological Science*, Vol. 18, No. 5, 2009, pp. 264–268.

Kelley, Thomas M., "Health Realization: A Principle-Based Psychology of Positive Youth Development," *Child & Youth Care Forum*, Vol. 32, No. 1, February 2003, pp. 47–72.

Kennedy, James E., Robert Davis, and Bruce Taylor, "Changes in Spirituality and Well-Being Among Victims of Sexual Assault," *Journal for the Scientific Study of Religion*, Vol. 37, No. 2, 2000, pp. 322–328.

Koenig, Harold G., "An 83-Year-Old Woman with Chronic Illness and Strong Religious Beliefs," *Journal of American Medical Association*, Vol. 288, No. 4, July 24/31, 2002, pp. 487–493. As of June 22, 2012: http://www.gvsu.edu/forms/ahf/JAMA%20July%2024,%202002.pdf

———, "Spirituality and Depression: A Look at the Evidence," *Southern Medical Journal*, Vol. 100, No. 7, July 2007, pp. 737–739.

———, "Concerns About Measuring 'Spirituality' in Research," *The Journal of Nervous and Mental Disease,* Vol. 196, No. 5, May 2008, pp. 349–355.

———, "Research on Religion, Spirituality, and Mental Health: A Review," *The Canadian Journal of Psychiatry* Vol. 54, No. 5, May 2009, pp. 283–291.

Koenig, Harold G., Dana E. King, and Verna B. Carson, *Handbook of Religion and Health, 2nd Edition,* Oxford: Oxford University Press, 2012.

Krause, Neal, "Exploring the Stress-Buffering Effects of Church-Based and Secular Social Support on Self-Related Health in Late Life," *Journal of Gerontology: Series B: Psychological Sciences & Social Sciences,* Vol. 61B, No. 1, 2006, pp. S35–S43.

Krause, Neal, Christopher G. Ellison, Benjamin A. Shaw, John P. Marcum, and Jason D. Boardman, "Church-Based Social Support and Religious Coping," *Journal for the Scientific Study of Religion,* Vol. 40, No. 4, December 2001, pp. 637–656.

LaRocca-Pitts, Mark, "Taking a Spiritual History in a Clinical Setting," *Journal of Health Care Chaplaincy,* Vol. 15, No. 1, 2008, pp. 1–12.

———, "In Fact, Chaplains Have a Spiritual Assessment Tool," *Australian Journal of Pastoral Care and Health,* Vol. 3, No. 2, December 2009, pp. 8–15. As of June 22, 2012:
http://www.pastoraljournal.findaus.com/pdfs/ar2.pdf

Leopold, Jason, "Army's 'Spiritual Fitness' Test Comes Under Fire," Truthout, January 5, 2011. As of February 21, 2013:
http://www.truth-out.org/news/item/268-army's-"spiritual-fitness"-test-comes-under-fire

Lewallen, Lynne Porter, "Commentary on the Provision of Spiritual Care by Registered Nurses on a Maternal–Infant Unit," *Journal of Holistic Nursing,* Vol. 27, No. 1, March 2009, pp. 29–30.

Lewis, Lisa M., "Spiritual Assessment in African-Americans: A Review of Measures of Spirituality Used in Health Research," *Journal of Religion and Health,* Vol. 47, December 20, 2008, pp. 458–475.

Lindberg, Deborah A., "Integrative Review of Research Related to Meditation, Spirituality, and the Elderly," *Geriatric Nursing,* Vol. 26, No. 6, 2005, pp. 372–377.

Litz, Brett T., Nathan Stein, Eileen Delaney, Leslie Lebowitz, William P. Nash, Caroline Silva, and Shira Maguen, "Moral Injury and Moral Repair in War Veterans: A Preliminary Model and Intervention Strategy," *Clinical Psychology Review,* Vol. 29, 2009, pp. 695–706.

Lynch, Thomas R., Alexander L. Chapman, M. Zachary Rosenthal, Janice R. Kuo, and Marsha M. Linehan, "Mechanisms of Change in Dialectical Behavior Therapy: Theoretical and Empirical Observations," *Journal of Clinical Psychology,* Vol. 62, No. 4, 2006, pp. 459–480.

Mabe, Alex P., and Allan M. Josephson, "Child and Adolescent Psychopathology: Spiritual and Religious Perspectives," *Child and Adolescent Psychiatric Clinics,* Vol. 13, 2004, pp. 111–125.

Maestas, Nicole, and Sarah Gaillot, *An Outcome Evaluation of the Success for Kids Program*, Santa Monica, Calif.: RAND Corporation, TR-575-1-SFK, 2010. As of June 22, 2012:
http://www.rand.org/pubs/technical_reports/TR575-1.html

Maltby, John, and Liza Day, "Spiritual Involvement and Belief: The Relationship Between Spirituality and Eysenck's Personality Dimensions," *Personality and Individual Differences,* Vol. 3, No. 2, January 2001, pp. 187–192.

Matheis, Elizabeth N., David S. Tulsky, and Robert J. Matheis, "The Relation Between Spirituality and Quality of Life Among Individuals with Spinal Cord Injury," *Rehabilitation Psychology,* Vol. 51, No. 3, 2006, pp. 265–271.

Maugans, Todd A., "The Spiritual History," *Archives of Family Medicine,* Vol. 5, No. 1, January 1996, pp. 11–16.

McCloy, Thomas M., and William H. Clover, "Value Formation at the Air Force Academy," in Charles C. Moskos and Frank R. Wood, eds., *The Military: More Than Just a Job?* Washington, D.C.: Pergamon-Brassey's, 1988, pp. 129–149.

McGene, Juliana, *Social Fitness and Resilience: A Review of Relevant Constructs, Measures, and Links to Well-Being*, Santa Monica, Calif.: RAND Corporation, RR-108-AF, 2013. As of October 2013:
http://www.rand.org/pubs/research_reports/RR108.html

McNulty, Kristy, Hanoch Livneh, and Lisa M. Wilson, "Perceived Uncertainty, Spiritual Well-Being, and Psychosocial Adaptation in Individuals with Multiple Sclerosis," *Rehabilitation Psychology,* Vol. 49, No. 2, 2004, pp. 91–99.

Meadows, Sarah O., and Laura L. Miller, *Airman and Family Resilience: Lessons from the Scientific Literature,* Santa Monica, Calif.: RAND Corporation, RR-106-AF, forthcoming.

Merrill, Ray M., and Richard Salazar, "Relationship Between Church Attendance and Mental Health Among Mormons and Non-Mormons in Utah," *Mental Health, Religion and Culture,* Vol. 5, No. 1, 2002, pp. 17–33.

Merrill, Ray M., Jeffrey Folsom, and Susan Christopherson, "The Influence of Family Religiosity on Adolescent Substance Use According to Religious Preference," *Social Behavior and Personality,* Vol. 33, No. 8, 2005, pp. 821–836.

Moberg, David O., "Research in Spirituality, Religion, and Aging," *Journal of Gerontological Social Work,* Vol. 45, No. 1, 2005, pp. 11–40.

Moreira-Almeida, Alexander, Francisco L. Neto, and Harold G. Koenig, "Religiousness and Mental Health: A Review," Rev*ista Brasileira de Psiquiatria,* Vol. 28, No. 3, September 2006, pp. 242–250.

Moskos, Charles C., "From Institution to Occupation: Trends in Military Organization," *Armed Forces & Society,* Vol. 4, No. 1, 1977, pp. 41–50.

Moskos, Charles C., and Frank R. Wood, "Institution Building in an Occupational World," in Charles C. Moskos and Frank R. Wood, eds., *The Military: More Than Just a Job?* Washington, D.C.: Pergamon-Brassey's, 1988, pp. 279–291.

Mullen, Admiral Michael, "On Total Force Fitness in War and Peace," *Military Medicine*, Vol. 175, Supplement 2010, pp. 1–2.

Nichols, Lindsey M., and Brandon Hunt, "The Significance of Spirituality for Individuals with Chronic Illness: Implications for Mental Health Counseling," *Journal of Mental Health Counseling,* Vol. 33, No. 1, January 2011, pp. 51–66.

Norton, Maria C., Archana Singh, Ingmar Skoog, Christopher Corcoran, JoAnn T. Tschanz, Peter P. Zandi, John C. S. Breitner, Kathleen A. Welsh-Bohmer, and David C. Steffens, "Church Attendance and New Episodes of Major Depression in a Community Study of Older Adults: The Cache County Study," *Journal of Gerontology: Psychological Sciences,* Vol. 63B, No. 3, 2008, pp. 129–137.

Olsthoorn, Peter, "Honor as a Motive for Making Sacrifices," *Journal of Military Ethics,* Vol. 4, No. 3, 2005, pp. 183–197.

———, "A Critique of Integrity: Has a Commander a Moral Obligation to Uphold His Own Principles?" *Journal of Military Ethics,* Vol. 8, No. 2, 2009, pp. 90–104.

Oman, Doug, Carl Thoresen, and John Hedberg, "Does Passage Meditation Foster Compassionate Love Among Health Professionals? A Randomised Trial," *Mental Health, Religion & Culture,* Vol. 13, No. 2, 2010, pp. 129–154.

Pace, Thaddeus W. W., Lobsang Tenzin Negi, Daniel D. Adame, Steven P. Cole, Teresa I. Sivilli, Timothy D. Brown, Michael J. Issa, and Charles L. Raison, "Effect of Compassion Meditation on Neuroendocrine, Innate Immune and Behavioral Responses to Psychosocial Stress," *Psychoneuroendocrinology,* Vol. 34, 2009, pp. 87–98.

Paloutzian, R. F., and C. W. Ellison, "Loneliness, Spiritual Well-Being, and the Quality of Life," in Letitia Anne Peplau and Daniel Perlman, eds., *Loneliness: A Sourcebook of Current Theory, Research and Therapy*, New York: Wiley Interscience, 1982.

Parameshwar, Sangeeta "Spiritual Leadership Through Ego-Transcendence: Exceptional Responses to Challenging Circumstances," *The Leadership Quarterly,* Vol. 16, 2005, pp. 689–722.

Paranjape, Anuradha, and Nadine J Kaslow, "Family Violence Exposure and Health Outcomes Among Older African American Women: Do Spirituality and Social Support Play Protective Roles?" *Journal of Women's Health,* Vol. 19, No. 10, November 10, 2010, pp. 1899–1904.

Pargament, Kenneth I., *Spiritually Integrated Psychotherapy: Understanding and Addressing the Sacred,* New York: The Guilford Press, 2007.

———, "The Sacred Character of Community Life," *American Journal of Community Psychology,* Vol. 41, 2008, pp. 22–34.

Pargament, Kenneth I., Bruce W. Smith, Harold G. Koenig, and Lisa Perez, "Patterns of Positive and Negative Religious Coping with Major Life Stressors," *Journal for the Scientific Study of Religion,* Vol. 37, No. 4, 1998, pp. 710–724.

Pargament, Kenneth I., Harold G. Koenig, Nalini Tarakeshwar, and June Hahn, "Religious Struggle as a Predictor of Mortality Among Medically Ill Elderly Patients," *Archives of Internal Medicine,* Vol. 161, August 13/27, 2001, pp. 1881–1885.

Peterson, Christopher, Nansook Park, and Carl A. Castro, "Assessment for the U.S. Army Comprehensive Soldier Fitness Program: The Global Assessment Tool," *American Psychologist,* Vol. 66, No. 1, 2011, pp. 10–18.

Rasic, Daniel T., Shay-Lee Belik, Brenda Elias, Laurence Y. Katz, Murray Enns, and Jitender Sareen, *Spirituality, Religion and Suicidal Behavior in a Nationally Representative Sample*, Winnipeg: University of Manitoba, 2009.

Richardson, Amy, Anita Chandra, Laurie T. Martin, Claude Messan Setodji, Bryan W. Hallmark, Nancy F. Campbell, Stacy Ann Hawkins, and Patrick Grady, *Effects of Soldiers' Deployment on Children's Academic Performance and Behavioral Health*, Santa Monica, Calif.: RAND Corporation, MG-1095-A, 2011. As of June 22, 2012: http://www.rand.org/pubs/monographs/MG1095.html

Riley, Barth B., Robert Perna, Denise G. Tate, Marty Forchheimer, Cheryl Anderson, and Gall Luera, "Types of Spiritual Well-Being Among Persons with Chronic Illness: Their Relation to Various Forms of Quality of Life," *Archives of Physical and Medical Rehabilitation,* Vol. 79, March 1998, pp. 258–264.

Robins, Clive J., "Zen Principles and Mindfulness Practice in Dialectical Behavior Therapy," *Cognitive and Behavioral Practice,* Vol. 9, 2002, pp. 50–57.

Robins, Clive J., and Alex L. Chapman, "Dialectical Behavior Therapy: Current Status, Recent Developments, and Future Directions," *Journal of Personality Disorders,* Vol. 18, No. 1, 2004, pp. 73–89.

Robson, Sean, *Physical Fitness and Resilience*: *A Review of Relevant Constructs, Measures, and Links to Well-Being*, Santa Monica, Calif.: RAND Corporation, RR-104-AF, 2013. As of October 2013:
http://www.rand.org/pubs/research_reports/RR104.html

———, *Psychological Fitness and Resilience: A Review of Relevant Constructs, Measures, and Links to Well-Being*, Santa Monica, Calif.: RAND Corporation, RR-102-AF, forthcoming.

Robson, Sean, and Nicholas Salcedo, *Behavioral Fitness and Resilience: A Review of Relevant Constructs, Measures, and Links to Well-Being*, Santa Monica, Calif.: RAND Corporation, RR-103-AF, forthcoming.

Rosenthal, Joshua Z., Sarina Grosswald, Richard Ross, and Norman Rosenthal, "Effects of Transcendental Meditation in Veterans of Operation Enduring Freedom and Operation Iraqi Freedom with Posttraumatic Stress Disorder: A Pilot Study," *Military Medicine,* Vol. 176, No. 6, 2011, pp. 626–630.

Rothman, Julie, "Spirituality: What We Can Teach and How We Can Teach It," *Journal of Religion and Spirituality in Social Work: Social Thought,* Vol. 28, No. 1, 2009, pp. 161–184.

Rushton, Philippe J., Roland D. Chrisjohn, and G. Cynthia Fekken, "The Altruistic Personality and the Self-Report Altruism Scale," *Journal of Personality and Individual Differences,* Vol. 22, March 26, 1981, pp. 293–302.

Scott, Eric L., Albert A. Agresti, and George Fitchett, "Factor Analysis of the 'Spiritual Well-Being Scale' and Its Clinical Utility with Psychiatric Inpatients," *Journal for the Scientific Study of Religion,* Vol. 37, No. 2, June 1998, pp. 314–321.

Sexson, Sandra B., "Religious and Spiritual Assessment of the Child and Adolescent," *Child and Adolescent Psychiatric Clinics,* Vol. 13, 2004, pp. 35–47.

Shapiro, Shauna, Doug Oman, Carl Thoresen, Thomas G. Plante, and Tim Flinders, "Cultivating Mindfulness: Effects on Well-Being," *Journal of Clinical Psychology,* Vol. 64, 2008, pp. 840–862.

Shih, Regina A., Sarah O. Meadows, and Margret T. Martin, *Medical Fitness and Resilience: A Review of Relevant Constructs, Measures, and Links to Well-Being,*

Santa Monica, Calif.: RAND Corporation, RR-107-AF, 2013. As of October 2013:
http://www.rand.org/pubs/research_reports/RR107.html

Shih, Regina A., Sarah O. Meadows, John Mendeloff, and Kirby Bowling, *Environmental Fitness and Resilience: A Review of Relevant Constructs, Measures, and Links to Well-Being,* Santa Monica, Calif.: RAND Corporation, RR-101-AF, forthcoming.

Smith, Bruce W., Erin M. Tooley, Erica Q. Montague, Amanda E Robinson, Cynthia J. Cosper, and Paul G. Mullinsy, "The Role of Resilience and Purpose in Life in Habituation to Heat and Cold Pain," *The Journal of Pain,* Vol. 10, No. 5, May 2009, pp. 493–500.

Soeters, Joseph L., "Value Orientations in Military Academies: A Thirteen Country Study," *Armed Forces & Society,* Vol. 24, No. 7, 1997, pp. 7–32.

Stanard, Rebecca Powell, Daya Singh Sandhu, and Linda C. Painter, "Assessment of Spirituality in Counseling," *Journal of Counseling & Development,* Vol. 78, 2000, pp. 204–210.

Storch, Eric A., Jonathan W. Roberti, Amanda D. Heidgerken, Jason B. Storch, Adam B. Lewin, Erin M. Killiany, Audrey L. Baumeister, Erica A. Bravata, and Gary R. Geffken, "The Duke Religion Index: A Psychometric Investigation," *Pastoral Psychology,* Vol. 53, No. 2, November 2004, pp. 175–181.

Suthers-McCabe, H. Marie, Elizabeth E. Van Voorhees, and Angela K. Fournier, *Psychosocial Impact of a Service Dog Training Program on Inmate Trainers*, Blacksburg, Va.: Center for Animal-Human Relationships, October 6–9, 2004.

Tanyi, Ruth A., "Towards Clarification of the Meaning of Spirituality," *Nursing Theory and Concept Development or Analysis,* Vol. 39, No. 5, May 2002, pp. 500–509.

Taylor, Elizabeth J., Iris Mamier, Khaled Bahjri, Triin Anton, and Floyd Petersen, "Efficacy of a Self-Study Programme to Teach Spiritual Care," *Journal of Clinical Nursing,* Vol. 18, 2008, pp. 1131–1140.

Tedeschi, Richard G., and Lawrence G. Calhoun, "The Posttraumatic Growth Inventory: Measuring the Positive Legacy of Trauma," *Journal of Traumatic Stress,* Vol. 9, No. 3, 1996, pp. 455–471.

Thompson, Brian L., and Jennifer Waltz, "Self-Compassion and PTSD Symptom Severity," *Journal of Traumatic Stress,* Vol. 21, No. 6, December 2008, pp. 556–558.

Travis, Fred, David A. F. Haaga, John Hagelin, Melissa Tanner, Sanford Nidich, Carolyn Gaylord-King, Sarina Grosswald, Maxwell Rainforth, and Robert H. Schneider, "Effects of Transcendental Meditation Practice on Brain Functioning and Stress

Reactivity in College Students," *International Journal of Psychophysiology,* Vol. 71, 2009, pp. 170–176.

Tsai, Jeanne L., and Emma Seppala, "Good Feelings in Christianity and Buddhism: Religious Differences in Ideal Affect," *Personality and Social Psychology Bulletin,* Vol. 33, No. 3, 2007, pp. 409–421.

Tshabalala, Bhekani G., and Cynthia J. Patel, "The Role of Praise and Worship Activities in Spiritual Well-Being: Perceptions of a Pentecostal Youth Ministry Group," *International Journal of Children's Spirituality,* Vol. 15, No. 1, 2010, pp. 73–82.

Tuck, Inez, Renee Alleyne, and Wantana Thinganjana, "Spirituality and Stress Management in Healthy Adults," *Journal of Holistic Nursing,* Vol. 24, No. 4, December 2006, pp. 245–253.

Underwood, Lynn G., and Jeanne A. Teresi, "The Daily Spiritual Experience Scale: Development, Theoretical Description, Reliability, Exploratory Factor Analysis, and Preliminary Construct Validity Using Health-Related Data," *The Society of Behavioral Medicine*, Vol. 24, No. 1, 2002, pp. 22–33.

Verweij, Desiree, Kim Hofhuis, and Joseph L. Soeters, "Moral Judgment within the Armed Forces," *Journal of Military Ethics,* Vol. 6, No. 1, 2007, pp. 19–40.

Wachholtz, Amy B., and Kenneth I. Pargament, "Is Spirituality a Critical Ingredient of Meditation? Comparing the Effects of Spiritual Meditation, Secular Meditation, and Relaxation on Spiritual, Psychological, Cardiac, and Pain Outcomes," *Journal of Behavioral Medicine,* Vol. 28, No. 4, 2005, pp. 369–384.

—————, "Migraines and Meditation: Does Spirituality Matter?" *Journal of Behavioral Medicine,* Vol. 31, 2008, pp. 351–366.

Wachholtz, Amy B., Michelle J. Pearce, and Harold G Koenig, "Exploring the Relationship Between Spirituality, Coping, and Pain," *Journal of Behavioral Medicine,* Vol. 30, 2007, pp. 311–318.

Werber, Laura, Margaret C. Harrell, Danielle M. Varda, Kimberly Curry Hall, Megan K. Beckett, and Stefanie Stern, *Deployment Experiences of Guard and Reserve Families: Implications for Support and Retention*, Santa Monica, Calif.: RAND Corporation, MG-645-OSD, 2008. As of June 22, 2012:
http://www.rand.org/pubs/monographs/MG645.html

Wiech, Katja, Miguel Farias, Guy Kahane, Nicholas Shackel, Wiebke Tiede, and Irene Tracey, "An FMRI Study Measuring Analgesia Enhanced by Religion as a Belief System," *Pain,* Vol. 139, 2009, pp. 467–476.

Wiist, W. H., B. M. Sullivan, H. A. Wayment, and M. Warren, "A Web-Based Survey of the Relationship Between Buddhist Religious Practices, Health, and Psychological

Characteristics: Research Methods and Preliminary Results," *Journal of Religion and Health,* Vol. 49, 2010, pp. 18–31.

Windham, R. Craig, Lisa M. Hooper, and Patricia E. Hudson, "Selected Spiritual, Religious, and Family Factors in the Prevention of School Violence," *Counseling and Values,* Vol. 49, 2005, pp. 208–216.

Yeung, Douglas, and Margret T. Martin, *Spiritual Fitness and Resilience: A Review of Relevant Constructs, Measures, and Links to Well-Being,* Santa Monica, Calif.: RAND Corporation, RR-100-AF, 2013. As of October 2013:
http://www.rand.org/pubs/research_reports/RR100.html

Made in the USA
Monee, IL
03 August 2021